THE PSYCHOANALYTIC DIALOGUE

The Psychoanalytic Dialogue

Stanley A. Leavy

Yale University Press
New Haven and London
1980

Designed by James J. Johnson
and set in Trump Medieval type.
Printed in the United States of America by
Edwards Brothers, Inc., Ann Arbor, Mich.

Published in Great Britain, Europe, Africa, and
Asia (except Japan) by Yale University Press,
Ltd., London, Distributed in Australia and
New Zealand by Book & Film Services, Artarmon,
N.S.W., Australia; and in Japan by Harper & Row,
Publishers, Tokyo Office.

Library of Congress Cataloging in Publication Data
Leavy, Stanley A   1915–
    The psychoanalytic dialogue.

    Bibliography: p.
    Includes index.
    1. Psychoanalysis.   2. Psychotherapist and
patient.   3. Interpersonal communication.
I. Title.
RC506.L4   616.8'917   79–21796
ISBN 0–300–02430–4

In one voyage
Did Claribel her husband find at Tunis,
And Ferdinand her brother found a wife
Where he himself was lost; Prospero his dukedom
In a poor isle; and all of us ourselves
When no man was his own.

The Tempest

Contents

Preface

The position of psychoanalysis is perennially ambiguous. Claims for it and criticisms of it have ranged widely, and it is hardly surprising that the uninitiated remain suspicious of it. To begin with, it was berated as a willful charlatanry or as the product, honest but misleading, of a benighted obsessional.[1] Almost from its beginnings, on the other hand, it commanded the fascinated respect of an official band of followers, and for all their deviations and defections, their innovations, and their inevitable enlargement and giving place to new generations, they have occupied a central and quasi-hierarchical status. The publication in English of the Standard Edition of Freud's psychological works proclaimed a *monumentum aere perennius* to the world, and at the same time an inerrant criterion of orthodox psychoanalytic thought. Advances in psychoanalysis ostensibly comparable to progress in natural sciences are based on hitherto unexplored or insufficiently appreciated aspects of Freud's thought. Sometimes even writers with theoretical views dia-

1. William James, who had a friendly attitude toward the concept of the unconscious, nevertheless considered such an epithet appropriate for Freud. See Perry 1935, vol. 2, p. 122–23.

metrically opposed to Freud's support them by making private interpretations of Freud's "real" intentions.[2]

We are not likely to get far from this fundamental innovator, it seems, and have much left of psychoanalysis. The great departures in the early days of psychoanalysis resulted in the establishment of new systems, which have either, in the case of Adler's, been more or less surreptitiously assimilated into Freudian analysis, or, in the case of Jung's, been discarded as a gnostic heresy with which a new conjunction is increasingly unlikely. Training in psychoanalysis is training in Freud's writings, under the instruction of a line of teachers who can prove their intellectual and academic descent from the early masters.

There is something in all this, as many have charged, of a religious order; there is also something in it of the transmission of an aesthetic doctrine. What exercises many minds, however, is the thought that such an adherence as this deserves that most damning of all modern execrations: it is *unscientific*. And consequently new voices from within psychoanalysis call for redefinitions of science that will not leave us outside.

The "science" issue is a crux, and legitimacy is all

2. Jacques Lacan makes the astonishing claim that Freud's anatomical-biological understanding of the instincts is not Freud's at all but "is built out of selections from the works of Freud" (Lacan 1977, p. 54). Even the most sympathetic reader of Lacan's transformation of Freud's biological concepts into symbolic ones must boggle at the anachronism that Lacan enlists to rescue Freud.

on one side. That terrible "tide of occultism," against which Freud warned Jung (Jung, 1963), seems to educated men and women to be a persistent menace, from which only scientific thinking can deliver us— for science alone can tell us about things as they are, uninfluenced by human illusions. There is a deep irony, one worthy of much more thought than we can give it here, in the state of psychoanalysis as at once a system that outlaws irrational, mystical, religious opinion and is itself looked on as exactly that. Let us leave that subject with only the hint that maybe the idea of science itself has undergone a degradation in becoming the primary center of value in the modern world rather than one of several.

In what follows I shall refer often to the problematic state of psychoanalysis. In fact I should say at the outset that I look on this as its permanent condition. No doubt all the accepted sciences undergo changes with the movement of emphasis from one superordinate hypothesis to another. It is much more likely that the study of the mind in general, and of the unconscious mind in particular, will be affected by currents in the intellectual life of the times. Fixity, stabilization, even predictability are as intellectual conditions the product of massive thought control; that they can be produced we know all too well, although we also draw comfort from the knowledge that there is something in the human spirit that ultimately rebels.

In this study I look at psychoanalysis concentratedly as a system of interpretation. In the first chapter

I examine some of the ideas regnant in medicine that prepared the way for Freud's concepts of interpretation, and then show how these concepts grew in Freud's work. In the second chapter I try to demonstrate the centrality of interpretation in all psychoanalytic work. The third chapter concentrates on the interaction of the patient and analyst in producing interpretations, and in the fourth this dialectical interchange is seen to be the heart of the process by which the past is recovered.

To concentrate is to exclude, and in such a small study it is easy to omit a great deal. Throughout the chapters I raise questions about the importance of much that has general recognition in official psychoanalytic quarters. I think that my own preferences are reasonably clear in most of these allusions, but I am aware that my arguments are only sketched. I am also aware that I leave myself open to the charge of inconsistency and even ingratitude when I pursue lines of thought that are far from original with me and for the existence of which I have to thank theoretical positions that I disclaim. For example, Paul Ricoeur, to whom I owe so much, has insisted that it is impossible to split off the hermeneutic (interpretive) side of psychoanalytic theory from the energetic, because the two are interdependent. I can readily concede that this was so in the development of Freud's thought, without being at all convinced that it is a necessary union any more. Nevertheless, I believe that what I have to say about interpretation ought to be no less valid even

if I am without allegiance to the theory of the libido
and to metapsychology as a whole.

Mention of Ricoeur brings me to the acknowledgement that I lean heavily on him and some other phen-
omenologist philosophers without having any proven
competence in their field. I work on the assumption
that philosophers do not, or should not, write only for
other philosophers, just as I appropriate the findings of
linguists without being one myself. I have little Heidegger, less Hegel, and no Husserl, and I hope I do not
use them to misunderstand them. But I have followed
them where they seemed pertinent and left them
where I could not follow them. Another philosopher,
my friend Edward Casey, has been unstintingly help-
ful in clarifying many of my ideas, but I hope that no
one will attribute my failings to him. I have been per-
suaded that the phenomenological task of trying to
understand interpretation as it is done is eminently
worthwhile, although a fully phenomenological account may not be possible, and certainly not by me. I
bring to it, however, something that only a practi-
tioner can bring, namely decades of active participation in the dialectical operations of psychoanalytic
practice.

Second only to my debt to this philosophical point
of view is that which I owe to Jacques Lacan. I have
already written sufficiently critically of many aspects
of his work to make it plain that I am not of his
school; I have simply followed my eclectic disposition
and have used his ideas when and where I could. From

all I know about him he would be in thorough disagreement with much that I hold to with respect to interpretation and might, if he took the trouble, place me among the unregenerate traditionalists. For all that, he remains, after allowance has been made for the exaggerations of his claims and pardon granted for the hopelessness of his style of communicating his ideas, the most important contributor to psychoanalysis in recent times. He is a genuine subversive and in this instance a much needed one; moving the basis of psychoanalysis from instinct to language was worth this French revolution, but Lacan's greatest contribution may prove to be the revolution itself,[3] the reopening of old concepts on a large scale.

The danger in any phenomenological account of psychoanalysis is the likelihood of trivialization, by substituting a simplistic empiricism for Freud's systematic theory. Let me state at the outset that I know that no accounting for mental life can be simple and still be faithful to experience. I have tried to focus my attention on what I conceive of as the foundation of the whole psychoanalytic enterprise—interpretation, and more specifically, interpretation of the unconscious meaning of that which is said in a psychoanalysis. I have attempted to make plain the theoretical position from which I work, as this is essential to any phenomenological view: if you do not know where I stand before I hear what I shall interpret, how can you estimate the distortion that I introduce? Or, to use a

3. For the historical background of Lacan's work see Turkle 1978.

less provocative word, how can you see the formal structure of my interpretations? But for all that, the drift of my approach is in a different direction: I am interested in the intensely personal nature of the psychoanalytic dialogue, even if it be at the expense of many important theoretical considerations. This also may mean to emphasize the humanistic at the expense of the scientific side of psychoanalysis, and within the humanistic to pay closest attention to the personalistic aspect. Freud's principal contribution to human life was to inaugurate a gigantic effort at exploration of the inaccessible fastnesses of the unconscious, but every step of the journey must be undertaken by way of the simplest of all human encounters, the dialogue.

Although I want to stress that this is the work of a clinician and that I have tried to say nothing in it that we analysts have not "proved upon our pulses"[4] — that is, seen in practice, I have not written a manual of interpretation. If any of my readers learn anything from me that will assist them in the work of interpretation, I shall be pleased to know it, but that kind of instruction is not my intention.

4. John Keats, in a letter to J. H. Reynolds, 27 April 1818.

Acknowledgments

Besides the writers to whose work I have expressed my indebtedness in the preface and elsewhere, I wish to thank my friends Darius Ornston and Warren Poland for their close and critical reading of the manuscript. I am under obligation to Jane Isay for encouraging me to put my thoughts into book form. My wife, Margaret, as always was the mainstay of my efforts. I would have had nothing to write about without my patients of many years who have contributed to the dialogue, and it is to them that this volume is gratefully dedicated.

1

Freud's Interpretive Method and Theory

The first psychoanalytic interpretation of which we have a definite record was made in March 1881 (Breuer and Freud, 1893–95, p. 25). It was given by Josef Breuer to a patient whom we know as "Anna O." and who had been mute for two weeks, during which she was "unable to say a syllable." Breuer told her then that she was offended about something and had determined not to speak about it. He wrote: "When I guessed this and obliged her to talk about it, the inhibition, which had made any other kind of utterance impossible as well, disappeared." We note that Breuer supposed that Anna had determined not to speak of something; that is, that she was or had been quite conscious of a resolution. She was apparently unaware of what Breuer "guessed": that in order to maintain silence about one thing, the offense, she had also determined, *unconsciously*, to remain silent about everything else as well. He told her that her muteness, not just her stubborn refusal to discuss her grievance, was of her own will. Whatever ideas Breuer had already formulated concerning the mechanisms of this mysterious hysterical process, the experiences involved could also be expressed in everyday terms: she was offended, and he guessed that she felt so. At the same time he also guessed that she had generalized her voluntary silence on one subject into a universal, unconsciously willed silence. He told her so, and then she could, or would, speak again. Simple as it now seems in long retrospect, the processes included a new idea, that silence willed for one intention might entail silence also willed for another, but without conscious awareness.

It is of course an arbitrary act to assign priority to this or any other of the recorded accounts of interpretations, and it is glaringly so in this instance, which historically precedes even the naming or the definition of psychoanalysis. Breuer then, and Freud a little later when he joined him in the work, used hypnosis and not the method of free association that is peculiar to psychoanalysis. In addition, as Freud was first to tell us, historical and literary works from many sources contain examples of interpretation of intentions of which someone, the subject of the interpretation, was unaware. In a rough commonsense way, interpretations of this kind are frequently enacted, and always have been, since human beings have been able to infer from their own self-consciousness what might be taking place in the minds of others. All that can be claimed for this instance is that it was made by a forerunner in the enunciation of the theory and method of psychoanalysis and that it was inseparable from a theory of unconscious mental processes. Another illustration might make the same point; the important thing is to try to see psychoanalytic interpretation in the setting of its explicit origins. Let us look at it more closely in respect to some of its details, and more broadly in respect to its background.

Part of the special interest of this interpretation is that it is seemingly not based on any act of speech at all. On the contrary it is based on a non-act, a non-speaking, on the part of someone who usually had a great deal to say. Taken in connection with what had gone on before, however, and granted the perspicacity of the observer, Anna's muteness was paradoxically an equivalent of speech. It was, to adapt the legal term, a "negative pregnant," from which, at that time and under those circumstances, a positive intention could be inferred. Anna might indeed have found other ways of expressing that intention than by a generalized silence. A witness who refuses to testify might conceal relevant evidence in other ways than by being silent: by lying perhaps, or by a more judicious form of equivocation obviating the charge of perjury. Anna in this instance might have continued to talk, while communicating her displeasure by direct or oblique reference, but she did not. Spoiled child that she seems to have been, she would not talk at all. Why then did Breuer not leave it at that, and ascribe her silence to a pique of which she was as conscious as any other child? It would have seemed to some to be the parsimonious choice. We must assume that Anna, too, found her own muteness a displeasure and gave some kind of evidence to Breuer that she did not herself know what she was being silent about. By such

an assumption we are able to accept Breuer's inference, and his diagnosis of "inhibition." If this is so,
then the first interpretation was one in which missing
words were supplied.

The analysis of this instance is incomplete on all
accounts if it is separated from the more general setting. Breuer's liberating remarks (as they proved to be
for the immediate sequel) were not those of a merely
wise and experienced man who could recognize the
subtleties of a pouting girl's behavior. He was an in-
ternist and a neurologist engaged as a physician in the
treatment of the sick and as a scientist looking for
medical, neurological explanations for the sickness of
his patients, as well as for nervous and mental phenomena in general. This setting, which was also
Freud's, gave a form to psychoanalysis, the only form
it has had, no more to be deplored or glorified than
any other historical setting, but one that needs to be
understood if we are to try to get at the meaning of
psychoanalytic interpretation.

If the traditional story is true, it was Charcot who
started in Freud's thinking the idea that hysterical
symptoms had a meaning. Charcot's comment that in
the hysteric, "c'est toujours la chose génitale" (Freud,
1914, p. 14) is an interpretive statement in itself.[1] The
convulsion, the paralysis, the trance represent something other than themselves. We cannot be entirely

---

1. The whole passage is distinctly revelatory of a threshold of discovery seen in retrospect.

sure that for Charcot at this moment "la chose génitale" had a mental referent. He might have meant no more than that some sexual substance produced symptoms. The occasion on which Freud overheard the statement speaks otherwise, however. Charcot was referring to the hysterical symptoms of a woman whose husband was impotent, and it would be difficult for even the most resolutely mechanistic of minds to conclude that there was no intended connection between an enforced sexual deprivation and a psychic experience. At all events Freud did make the connection, and he lamented that the great French master of neurology in his public statements stuck to his explanations of what happened in hysteria in terms of cerebral anatomical changes—but Freud, for a while, did the same.

For all Freud's complaint about Charcot, he too fully accepted the medical horizons within which both of them worked. Scientific medicine differentiates symptoms from causes; it assigns symptoms to causes and it sternly prescribes that treatment be directed to causes and not to symptoms, although the practice of medicine may be quite different. A symptom may be visible and known medically as a "sign" or only be reported as a subjective event, but in either case a fully medical interpretation of it assigns it to a cause which is like the causes of physical disease. If the cause can be established to be itself physical then it has physical mediations, or at least its characteristics can be best understood as analogous to physical causes. Where Freud took the giant step was not to abandon the doctrine of causality, but to extend it to a new reach: the symptom did not need a physical process to explain it, like tumor or inflammation. The cause might be an event. "Trauma," originally purely physical, meaning a wound, might now designate a causal event, but as an event it is a historical explanation: the patient is ill because something happened in the past, and what happened had a mental significance from the beginning.[2] If it did not, how then would it be different from any other precipitating event, a fall, a blow, an infection, any of which also might make its full effect known after a period of "incubation"?

The idea of a medical history itself long antedates any psychological explanations. As soon as illness is observed as a temporal phenomenon, it is explained with respect to antecedent events. *Post hoc, ergo propter hoc,* may be bad reasoning very often, but the sequential nature of the events of illness demands some kind of historical explanation, and incorrect explanations, even of the wildest kind, are often preferred to no explanation. I do not know how far back into antiquity we have to go to find the first statement of the notion that every illness has a history. If we restrict

2. It was from Charcot that Freud took the name if not the concept of trauma, and for Charcot the word meant originally a physical injury, one which had a psychical effect. (See Freud, 1893, p. 27). For Freud as well as Breuer, the trauma was very early established as an event that need not be in any way physical, but that became the occasion for repression. Again, for example, Freud calls such a trauma "an occurrence of incompatibility" or an "experience, an idea, or a feeling, which aroused such a distressing affect that *the subject decided to forget about it*" (Freud 1893, p. 47).

ourselves arbitrarily again to the classical world, we find case histories not too different from our own from the fifth century B.C., as written by Hippocrates of Cos and his school. In such a case history, the writer puts down an account of what has happened to a sufferer from the moment he has first seen him or her until the outcome of the illness, which with Hippocrates' patients, as reported in the third book of *Epidemics* (Jones, 1923), was usually death. The history might also include an account by the patient or his relatives of presumably relevant events that preceded the first meeting of patient and physician.

In the case history as we have it written down, we read about two persons, the more manifest one being the sufferer, or patient, and the more concealed one the observer, or physician. A patient is in fact so called because his being is defined in the narrative by the illness, which he is required to endure, however involuntarily, as long as it persists. (This is also true when, as in the Greek language, the word for patient derives from a quite different root, one that does not in itself imply enduring as the Latin root *pati* does.) The physician is by name and in fact a student of *physis*, of nature, by which is intended not only the biological and cosmological world and its subspecies the world of human pathology, but more particularly the nature of this sufferer. "Physician" is our word and not Hippocrates', although as one of his translators concludes, in his writings "he has laid aside the part of the healer to be for a time a spectator looking down on the arena, exercising that θεωρία which a Greek held to be the highest human activity" (Jones, 1923, p. 144). His more primitive word *iatros*, meaning healer, shows the direction of thought that also conditions all medical science. Hippocrates' reports notwithstanding, the physician does not merely observe carefully what the patient is enduring. He tries to influence the patient by interfering with the illness. But the student of nature is always there, and it is sometimes poignantly clear that Hippocrates distinguished between the external natural circumstances and the human nature of the sufferer.

At least as early as Hippocrates' time, it was recognized that human nature is not limited to that which can be observed by the examination of the body. Human nature is historical, and the first part of the examination, then as now, consisted of a history, an *anamnesis* as it is still called, which means a calling to mind of a person's past. Nor did Hippocrates make this anamnesis just a listing of earlier symptoms or earlier diseases; it is also an account of his experiences, so far as they are thematically pertinent. For example, and much to our purpose, in case 11 of the third book of *Epidemics* (Jones, 1923, p. 277), he reported that "in Thasos a woman of gloomy temperament, after a grief with a reason for it [*ek lupes meta prophasies*], without taking to bed lost sleep and appetite, and suffered thirst and nausea," and so on. Note that the physician observed that she was disposed to gloominess and that she had been seriously and appropriately afflicted by a recent grief. Perhaps the most important comment, from our point of view, is that the grief was "with a reason," implying as it does that the father of western medicine knew about unreasonable grief too. That he looked on the event of the grief as part of a causal sequence is plain, and in the same way as he defined the physical cause of the plague, although lacking any knowledge of microbial infection.

In a sense the patient and the healer–observer were not the only two participants in the history. There was also the illness, which being itself substantialized, seemed to have a life of its own. If it was no longer, as it was by Homer's heroes, actually personified as the god Apollo with his murderous arrows, it was still a process, known by an "etiology." It had a cause, a course, that might be predictable, an outcome, and in the event of the survival of the patient sequelae or aftereffects following the recovery. This series of events that we are now able to relate to the interaction of human bodies with invading organisms introduced into the history of the patient an impersonal entity, itself fundamentally responsible for the suffering he or she reported or demonstrated.

As early then as the fifth century B.C. the dichotomous status of the explanation of symptoms prevailed within the case history. The substantialized illness is a thing, originating in an event, no less so when the causal event was reduced from the supernatural intervention of Apollo to the maleficent influence of "airs, waters, places," as another of Hippocrates' works is entitled, and it maintains this objectivized condition throughout. But we see in the touching instance of the woman of Thasos something of another kind too: there was indeed an event of a grief in the sense of the death or departure of a loved person, but there was also an experience, a grief in the sense of an affective state consequent to that death or loss and with psychosomatic symptoms as well. The patient cannot be fully described only in terms of the natural history of diagnosed illness occurring in a specific person. She also has a history of her own, her *story*. Both need to be interpreted in the treatment of the sick.

All this lies in the distant past, quite remote from our psychoanalytic science. If we are to make much of the history of the person in psychoanalytic interpretation, then we must also give due weight to the history of the idea of interpretation, and this is an essential part of it. The medical neurological basis of psychoanalysis gave it the direction it took in Freud's hands. Scientific medicine went through many changes in the long period between Hippocrates and Freud, but the elementary distinctions between sufferer, healing observer, and illness remained, and of course remain to the present. After all, of the three, only the illness is unmistakably a judgment rather than a concrete object. Patient and physician are self-existent individuals—not as such, however, but by virtue of the roles in which certain individuals are cast.[3] But despite the

3. Despite the long history of the patient–physician relationship, it remains a pair of signifiers, of attributions. It arises certainly out of a real state of affairs, the dis-ease of one person and the claim to therapeutic effectiveness of the other. But an equally accurate picture of shamanist

fact that the history of medicine is littered with the wrecks of established convictions, scientific medicine is the best we have for the prevention, management, and cure of illness, and it is where psychoanalysis began.

The treatment of Anna O., with which as I have suggested psychoanalytic interpretation began, is in direct continuity of tradition with the treatment of the woman of Thasos. The Greek physician was not called on to treat the "nervous" symptoms of the patient as Breuer was of his, but Breuer approached his patient from the same point of view of the professional discipline that above all looks to scientific demonstration and to confirmation of its claims. It operates through the authority of the "doctor"—the learned man—by which he induces patients to undertake often unpleasant, costly, or even dangerous remedies. He needs to believe in the correctness of his diagnosis and his prescription. Diagnosis is itself the interpretation in scientific medicine. It is intrinsic that both the sign and that which it signifies have substantive referents. Even when the interpretation leads to a historical event, first consideration is given to the objectivity, the reality of the event. I start from these considerations in examining, although only briefly, the development of the idea of interpretation in Freud's work.

I shall begin this examination by referring at some length to an admirable summary of the subject under-

treatment is based on other signifiers. (See, for example, Lévi-Strauss, 1967.)

taken by Didier Anzieu. It remains strictly within the boundaries of modern psychoanalytic theory, and for the most part avoids the critical questions with which we shall be largely concerned in this essay, but that does not make it less useful for us. Anzieu summarizes Freud's conceptions of interpretation as follows:

At the end of his self-analysis, Freud held that interpretation is that which explains but which is basically in no need of explanation itself. Interpretation is of the same nature as that which it interprets. It passes backward in time across successive layers of the past, like the archaeologist or the geologist. It recovers in the unconscious the "archives arranged in order" as in *Studies in Hysteria*. It lifts barriers to passage, and it unties knots. The requisite for the psychoanalyst's correct use of interpretation is that he know the theory of the function of the psychic apparatus in general and the specific processes of every psychoneurosis. It suffices for him to apply this knowledge correctly to the particular cases he undertakes to treat: interpretation is reduced to an art, from this point of view. It has no other content than that which is contained in the neurosis. . . . Unhappily, Freud was soon disenchanted: this correspondence, this homology, this connaturality are not confirmed by psychoanalytic practice. Freud had to think of interpretation no longer in impersonal and rationalized terms as a relation between the conscious and the unconscious by way of the preconscious, but in the dialectical, or better still the strategic perspective of a joust, or a "game of chess" between the psychoanalyst and the patient [1970, p. 778].

That is, the movement from the relatively simplistic view of analysis as excavation, to an elaborate dialectical process was absolutely necessitated once the Oedipus complex was recognized.[4] Once due attention was paid to the Oedipus complex, psychoanalytic interpretation became the interpretation of the Oedipus complex wherever, whenever, and however it appeared, to the degree of its resolution or nonresolution. Since this complex is the result of a dialectical process, the exchanges between parents and child, interpretation of it through transference became the key to psychoanalytic understanding.

It is striking all the same that as Anzieu sees it, the "archaeological method," which is really only the extension of the medical quest for objective causes into the psychic realm (the latter being imagined as a kind of time-binding space, bearing definable strata), leads to its own breakdown. Freud discovered the Oedipus complex by means of the archaeological method, and conceived of it as a causal agency, but it turned out that the dialectical process which comprised it was repeated in the treatment. I quote again from Anzieu's description of how this takes place:

The unconscious representation, pathogenic image or idea no longer necessarily corresponds with a repressed memory, but with the realization of a desire: it is the "fantasy." But

4. Anzieu here introduces the term "dialectical." Since it will recur in what follows, my use of it deserves definition: "Dialectics" cannot be wholly deprived of its technical or philosophic connotations, but I would like to use it rather loosely as a process of arriving at a conclusion (not necessarily definitive) through the confrontation of differing views. It is a process of exchange, cognitive and affective, and it implies absolutely the presence of individuals, two or more, who interact.

the fantasy appears now to have only a secondary role in itself, because it is determined by the play of cathexes bound to the subject's instinctual economy. By reactivating the drives, the psychoanalytic situation mobilizes and liberates fixated cathexes. The transference is the specific medium through which this reactivation operates. It restores life to the desires and to the fantasies in which the desires are expressed. Through the transference, change is effected by displacing the cathexis from one object to another, displacing it on to the analyst as the object of fantasy, and subsequently to other real external objects [1970, p. 782].

The last comments in this quotation are familiar enough explanatory concepts and have been handled with particular conviction by Loewald (1960) in his classical study of the therapeutic action of psychoanalysis, but here we see them in the setting of an account of the nature of interpretation. Most to the point are Anzieu's ideas that it is the transference, rather than the interpretation that effects the therapeutic transformation. This disjunction, often intended but not always so plainly stated, makes the transference, like the cathexes that allegedly are at bottom responsible for it, really in existence apart from the dialectical exchanges of the analysis, and this despite Anzieu's own acknowledgement that it is interpretation that brings about transference. In any case it is interpretation of the transference, not its supposed transcendental existence apart from the exchanges, that makes therapeutic transformations possible.

Logically enough, Anzieu then goes on to outline

the libido theory as part of his analysis of the interpretive process. Through interpretation, he says, the repression is lifted and libidinally cathected choices and goals may find their way to expression hitherto denied them by the repression and its symptomatic sequels. While the analytic process and not the analyst himself makes the changes possible, it is nevertheless the interpreting analyst who undoes the repression through the interpretation of the transference. Strachey's (1935) concept of "mutative" interpretation stresses this too. The analytic process reproduces the mother–infant relation (or so we have come to interpret our experiences in analyzing), and in addition to the old desires of infancy the anxieties of infancy are revived, based as they are on infinite longings for help, caring, and love, and the existential certainty of their not being gratified. Interpretation from the patient's point of view is first a voice to listen to and only thereafter a signifying word. Here Anzieu, once again close to Loewald's thought, finds the basis of interpretation in personal prehistory: the interpretation of the transference is driven back into the preverbal epoch and becomes "reconstructive" in a very real sense, dealing as it does in words with events that never had verbal representation.

While this "second theory" of interpretation in Freud's writings depends on the libido theory and the transference, Anzieu now finds a third theory following upon the enunciation of the death instinct, as it is identified with the repetition compulsion. He is in accord with Bibring's reading of the repetition compulsion as not only a movement "beyond the pleasure principle" but also a movement to restore the conditions antecedent to the "trauma." We note here once more how this contemporary of ours among historians of the growth of Freud's theory of interpretation, along with most later analysts, sees an ever-increasing shift of emphasis in Freud's ideas. He kept moving, it seems, from the position that the analyst is essentially a Hippocratic physician, exposing and objectifying the trauma, or the complex, as another physician might demonstrate the objectively present infection or tumor, to the recognition of something quite different, two experiencing and communicating individuals, in an interaction where they do not unearth buried strata, but revive exchanges. Anzieu goes further still: he concludes his study with the interesting comparison of the analyst's interpretations with those of the musical performer or conductor, who "keeps the notes, respects the melody and the text, but hears them in his own way and tries to get them heard in his own way." At this point the scientific observer has himself, or herself, been transformed.

Let us now look at Freud's introduction to the technique of interpretation in one of the earliest references made to it, that in the *Interpretation of Dreams* (1900). In a very familiar passage, Freud relates his method of interpreting dreams to the examination of the patient's free associations, which he had come to rely on in the interpretation of symptoms. The "archaeological" method here shines in the simplicity of its beginnings: "If a pathological idea . . . can be traced back to the elements in the patient's mental life from which it originated, it simultaneously crumbles away and the patient is freed from it."[5] One is reminded of Schliemann's excavations at Mycenae that unearthed in one place actual human tissues in addition to bone buried 3000 years, which began to vanish almost immediately on exposure to air. Applied to the dream this meant that the dream itself could be treated as a symptom, and its manifest content interpreted as the recent phases of a psychical chain that has to be traced backward in the memory.

A remarkable quotation from Schiller on literary productivity is included in Freud's account of the method of free association on which the practice of interpretation depends (it is also strikingly similar to very nearly contemporary opinions of John Keats about which I have written elsewhere [Leavy, 1970], and indeed it is part of the philosophic tradition of the romantic era), and it describes the method with a disarming clarity. "Looked at in isolation, a thought may seem very trivial or very fantastic; but it may be made important by another thought that comes after it, and in conjunction with other thoughts that may seem equally absurd, it turns out to form a most effective link" (Freud, 1900, p. 103). Schiller here is, of course, not archaeologizing, not uncovering the remote origins of a pathological idea or any other idea, but is suppos-

5. I shall discuss the great archaeological analogies at length in chapter 4. (Here see Freud 1900, p. 100.)

ing that the unchecked flow of ideas might yield unintended meaning. It is a matter of some moment that
Freud offered this quotation—which Otto Rank in
fact discovered for him—as prescriptive for his method,
which he had designed earlier under the influence of
Breuer's teachings. For there is a difference between
the relatively mechanistic notion of a chain of ideas
leading step by step back into the past, and this one of
influencing one idea by the approximation of another.
It is in fact analogous to the difference between the
presentation of a series of colors in a spectrum, and,
conversely, their appearance when they are artisti-
cally related to one another in a painting, so that their
mutual influences affect the observer. The method of
free association resembles the latter, and it is indeed
by inferences from the unintended (in a conscious
way) approximation of seemingly unrelated ideas that
Freud, and all later analysts, find their way to the
"buried memories," as we will illustrate in another
place.

Two other comments on this passage from *The
Interpretation of Dreams* are apposite here, although
to contrary purposes. First let us be reminded of the
footnote in which Freud, having just established the
propriety of the use of his own dreams in illustration
of his theory, now makes the avowal that he has not,
out of reasons of discretion, made a complete interpretation of any of his dreams (Freud, 1900, p. 105n). This
admission has prompted later writers to reanalyze
some of Freud's published dreams, and to offer interpretations in addition to his, some of them of a star-

tlingly revelatory nature. Since this procedure has been acceptable to such masters of our science as Erik Erikson (1954) and Max Schur (1966), we need not here quarrel with its appropriateness. But it is to the point that they could, on the basis of information obtained from other sources, infer some of the suppressed associations, and from these inferences reach their new interpretations. The theoretical import of the reanalyses of Freud's dreams lies not in their correctness, however, nor in their psychobiographical interest, but in the clear implication that the meaning of a dream changes with the increment of new associations to it. In this case the new associations were only presumptive, and they were attributable to the analyst of his own dreams, but we have to extend the principle to the interpretation of all dreams, and indeed of all statements; in brief, psychoanalytic interpretations are the joint product of the associations of the analysand and the analyst. Just as clearly as the example of the Oedipus complex asserted by Anzieu, the interpretation of dreams illustrates the dialectical nature of the process of interpretation in general.

On the other hand, the same chapter of Freud's greatest contribution to psychoanalysis points in another direction, the direction that has understandably come to be the dominant one whenever psychoanalytic theory is under discussion. We only occasionally read or hear of this theory as one based on the process of interpretation, until quite recently, since semiology has begun to come into its own. Freud's commitment to his grand physicalist analogy long antedates the dream book and is to be found in the writings of which Breuer was co-author. Here, in discussing free association, Freud quite naturally, and with no apology for speculation, moved from a description of the differences, verbal and behavioral, between the "reflecting" (that is, cogitating) person and the freely associating one, with the explanation that in the latter we see "the establishment of a psychical state which, in its distribution of psychical energy (*that is, of mobile attention*) bears some analogy to the state before falling asleep" (1900, p. 102). I have added emphasis to the parenthesized words because they set up at the beginning of the work in question a fateful equation: attention equals energy. Moreover the basis for the contention is present in the immediately foregoing sentences of Freud's: evidence is to be found in the "tense looks and wrinkled forehead of a person pursuing his reflections as compared with the restful expression of a self-observer." In free association, he goes on, the patient "employs the psychical energy thus saved (or a portion of it) in attentively following the involuntary thoughts which now emerge." The basic Freudian energetic theory, first laid down in the suppressed "Project" and fully sketched in the seventh chapter of *The Interpretation of Dreams* is here present in a nutshell, and, what is to our present purpose, it is presented as inseparable from the theory of interpretation. Indeed, it might be put that the energetic theory explains interpretation as if it were for Freud the necessary scientific link between what might otherwise appear to be a form of oneiromancy and the world of objective reality.

How this works may be made a little plainer by recalling the words of Didier Anzieu: What the chain of ideas leads to in Freud's "second theory" of interpretation is not necessarily the repressed memory but "the realization of a desire: it is the 'fantasy.' But the fantasy appears now to have a secondary role in itself, because it is determined by the play of cathexes bound to the subject's instinctual economy." In a word, the fantasies are epiphenomenal.

Curiously enough, references to the energetic explanation of interpretation are very scanty in the rest of Freud's book, until we come to the seventh chapter. It is called "The *Psychology* of the Dream-Processes," and Freud stubbornly resisted any attempt to reduce the theory of the dream to a nonpsychological explanation. But on the other hand Freud envisioned a smoother transition between psychological and neurological explanation than many others are capable of making, for either his energetics rests on an ultimate reduction to a biological system, or it floats in the air. Ricoeur (1970, p. 88) states that in *The Interpretation of Dreams*, "the systematic explanation is placed at the end of the work whose rules have been elaborated; the express aim of the explanation is to present a schematic transcription of what goes on in the dreamwork that is accessible only in and through the work of interpretation." Nevertheless, the work of interpretation as Freud analyzes it, with his repeated references to "psychic intensities," cries out for explanation. For Freud, as Ricoeur also shows, it was not the unconscious processes that were themselves unclear, but the ways in which they became conscious. Freud's method is in this way antiphenomenological, in that he tries to show how unconscious registrations, which are primary, can ever be transcribed as conscious ones (Ricoeur, 1970, p. 122).

In a tightly woven argument based largely on Freud's paper "The Unconscious," Ricoeur shows how Freud's theory of affects stands in the way of any complete assimilation of psychoanalytic process to hermeneutics. To the extent that meaning is reducible to transpositions of affects, or rather to the instinctual cathexes of which affects are the discharges, the "language of meaning" can never supersede the "language of force." But, and this is essential also, affects cathect ideas, forces are "in search of meaning," and therefore the interpretive side of psychoanalysis cannot be fully reduced to an economics either (Ricoeur, 1970, p. 149).

I believe that Ricoeur is right in understanding Freud in this fashion, but he also appears to follow Freud in his fidelity to a model of thought derived from the physical sciences that Ricoeur himself in a later and equally significant part of his book shows to be impossible.[6] Let us, however, leave this discussion,

6. See book 3, chapter 1, of Ricoeur's work. This section, which may be read separately from the whole, is a clear and persuasive account of the status of psychoanalysis as a science. It will not be acceptable to those who persist in the belief that the data of psychoanalysis lend themselves to the

and return to Freud's interpretive method as he prescribed it.

Outside of *The Interpretation of Dreams*, Freud is
remarkably uninformative with respect to his method
of interpretation. The papers dealing with technique,
on close reading, seem to slide over this particular operation, deservedly detailed as they are in such matters as the handling of the transference. We catch
vivid glimpses of Freud's pedagogic intentions when,
for example, he so clearly urges that the psychoanalyst through his "evenly suspended attention" provide
a "counterpart to the fundamental rule" followed by
the patient, and accounts for this in terms of the
"bending" of the analyst's unconscious toward the
emerging unconscious of the patient (Freud, 1912, pp.
111, 115). Where he leaves us unsatisfied is in regard
to the way this encounter between the unconscious of
the analyst and the unconscious of the analysand actually takes place.

There is more than a hint at a phenomenological—
as opposed to an energetic—account of this process
however still within the *Interpretation of Dreams*. In
it Freud is first actually explaining the temporal connections in dreams:

In a psychoanalysis one learns to interpret propinquity in
time as representing connection in subject matter. Two

kind of treatment present in the natural sciences. Unlike some of the other
philosophical criticism of psychoanalysis as science, however, Ricoeur's
does not in any way dismiss its commitment to truth. Instead, he argues
for consideration of psychoanalysis within the horizons of the intersubjective situation where it exists.

thoughts which occur in immediate sequence without any apparent connection are in fact part of a single unity which has to be discovered; in just the same way, if I write an "a" and a "b" in succession, they have to be pronounced as a single syllable "ab" [1900, p. 247].

And later, still with respect to dream interpretation,

Whenever [dreams] show us two elements close together, this guarantees that there is some especially intimate connection between what corresponds to them among the dream-thoughts [1900, p. 314].

It is fully consonant with the rest of Freud's theory to extend these comments to a general application, as he himself does in the "Dora" case. Every psychoanalytical interpretation has in principle the same form as that given for the connections established in dream interpretation. When someone says "a" and then "b," he or she unconsciously (metonymically) intends to say "ab." We hope for a larger number of integers than two in the series that constitute the unconscious structure, and we look for confirmation of the interpretation in the repeated appearance of such series with the same configuration. Further we attach peculiar significance to the series of integers when reference to the analyst, as second participant in the dialogue, is apparent. We find such interpretations most useful—maybe only then—when we can see in the structure "ab" reference to at least two other figures, the third being another aspect of the speaker than the present subject and the fourth another person than the present person of the analyst, as Lacan (1977, p. 139) has developed Freud's formulations.

A single idea, however laden with feelings, does not by itself reveal the unconscious—the exception being the "symbol" in Freud's sense, which we interpret warily, however, because symbols turn out to be polysemous like other signifiers and find their pertinent value, also like other signifiers, in the company they keep.[7]

As we shall see, the statement that contiguous or relatively proximate ideas (when I mention "ideas" I do not mean affectless ideas, which do not exist) taken together imply unconsciously intended structure is of course not subject to any kind of objective proof. Practical confirmation is all that we can get, through the repetition of latent structure, through new verbal contiguities, through actions reducible to language, through the evocation of suppressed memories, or through the elucidation of hitherto unclear memories.

7. I shall take up the linguistic theory of the signifier in chapter 3.

2

Toward Interpretation

When I had practiced psychoanalysis for about twenty years, I began to ask myself, more urgently than before, what I was doing. I had come to see the possibilities and the limitations of the work as I did it and as my colleagues did it, but I thought that I needed to inquire more deeply into its nature than I had done before, whether in my schooling long ago or in the study that I had done in the interval. I had early been convinced by demonstration in myself and others that we analyze in order to disclose unconscious mental content, which has the power so long as it remains undisclosed of binding the patient-to-be in constraints, of which he cannot be aware and which may run contrary to his avowed or avowable intentions. I had no quarrel with that accounting, but I did want to understand better how it came about that what I was doing could serve to disclose unconscious mental content, and even more I wanted to know what such content might be and what sort of view of mind such an idea presupposed.

The difficulty with the explanatory theory that began with Freud's "Project" (1954) was not that it used metaphors (like my word "constraints") or indeed that the whole system depended on a grand analogy, according to which mental processes were to be understood as being like transfers of energy, like neuronal exchanges. It is impossible to explain anything without the use of metaphor, unless one limits oneself to the uninteresting range within which symbolic logic is effective. Furthermore, as Loewald (1971) and others have remarked, some of the most accepted terms of physical science, which Freud applied to psychoanalytic theory, had their origin in descriptions of human interaction: "force," for example, which it might be said psychoanalysis merely had borrowed from physical science and restored it to its originally mental or at least behavioral meaning. The use of analogy is legitimate when it can be shown that the operations prevailing in one system consistently mirror those prevailing in another. To describe mental systems as systems of energy, bound and free, libidinal and aggressive, arranged so as to equip an armature of mind structured as ego, id, and superego, which in its adaptive flexibility could stand confronting the rest of the world and also be divided in itself, is both reasonable and interesting, and as developed over many decades by Freud, it is a lasting theoretical masterpiece.

My difficulty with all this lay elsewhere. I had found, in practice, that "psychoanalysis is interpretation from beginning to end" (Ricoeur, 1970, p. 66). In fact it was also evident that Freud's explanatory system was itself the result of a series of interpretations, some of which we have already referred to. The theory is an attempt to interpret the interpretations, but

what about the act of interpreting itself—is it inde-
pendent of theoretical considerations? Of course not.
It cannot be so, because we cannot entertain experiences without any presuppositions, without any pre-
structuring of reality. The irreducibly minimum concept of psychoanalysis as a theory or as a method is
the concept of the unconscious; whether that is taken
substantively as Freud's prevailing metaphoric use
does, or functionally, as MacIntyre (1958), in his philosophical critique of Freud, and Schafer (1976) both
urge, is not decisive. The interpretations made by psychoanalytic method differ from any other kind of
interpretations because their referents are unconscious; second, it is also essential that these unconscious referents be recognized as not mere parallels of
conscious thoughts, but as operatively existing in a
"second state." The discovery of the unconscious preceded psychoanalysis, not only in the writings of
many philosophic thinkers, but also in the clinical
practice of the specialists in hypnosis with whom
Freud worked, notably Bernheim, two of whose vol-
umes Freud translated into German.

Even the explanation of the execution of a post-
hypnotic suggestion is a kind of interpretation. When
the subject obeys the command to open the umbrella
inside the room and lamely rationalizes the act, we
explain it as one determined by a command previ-
ously issued, and not recalled in the present consciousness of the subject. It takes less stretching of the
phenomena to infer that the command has existed
and still exists in a second, unconscious state not fur-

ther describable in mental terms, than to attribute the act to a conscious compliance that is not acknowledged as such. As a matter of fact, the latter explanation, or the like one that invokes deliberate falsification on the part of the subject, also invokes the concept of the unconscious at another level. Freud, then, came to psychoanalysis with a concept of the unconscious that simultaneously requires interpretation and makes further interpretations possible. It is also a concept that is a statement about the nature of man as definitive as any biological concept.

Granted, then, that psychoanalytic interpretation will always have the unconscious as its matrix, what else is peculiar about it? It was in replying to this question that I found that we stood on different ground from Freud's, or, perhaps he stood on ground other than that he presumed to exist. Contrary to the traditional medical-biological view that Freud both inherited and transmitted, I became convinced that psychoanalytic interpretation has its ground in the dialogue between persons.

A person differs from any other "object" in that it is a person alone whom I address as "you."[1] As soon

1. The philosophical distinction between "I-Thou" and "I-It" lies deep, but it first came to my notice in the work of Martin Buber "I and Thou" (1937). It is important to recognize, in view of the widespread and confusing use of the term "object-relations," that Freud did not mean by "object" the reduction of the existence of a person to that of an impersonal thing. The whole value of an "object" in the Freudian sense is that it is a "thou," another subjective being; else how could the projection onto "objects" of hostile sentiments or the expectation of loving ones come into a person's mind?

as I recognize that, I can see that my explanations
with regard to persons must be fundamentally different from any other explanations. To be sure I can see
that mental life has enough repetitions and replica-
tions that we can know psychological laws, which at
least seem to stand on all fours with physical and biological laws. None of these is the discovery of psychoanalysis to the extent that they are laws—predictive
statements. They are the discoveries of empirical psychology, from the mindless psychophysics of Fechner
to the developmental psychology of Piaget. They have
relevance to psychoanalysis, since all have to do with
mental life, but they have probably not much more
relevance than neurological laws, which also define
the limits within which mental life can exist. Psychoanalytical discoveries, all bearing on the status of
unconscious mental life, grew out of the psychoanalytical situation, one in which the primary effort is at
interpretation, the discovery of meaning and intention.

Meaning, and the interpretive process through
which meaning is disclosed, exists in dialogue. I refer
of course only to personal meaning; we justifiably use
the word in nonpersonal situations, as astronomers
might when they look for the meaning of an unexpected mark on a photographic plate. Astronomers
will not ask the plate what it means, although they
may ask one another, in trying to explain the mark.
When we interpret personal meaning, we must ask
one another, for this kind of meaning exists between

us, even when it has another person, or a nonhuman
object as its third term. To be sure, on the way to understanding the meaning of something mental, we
may need to consider it as "it": the obsessive thought,
for example, exists as "it," and it is through interpretation that we hope to convert it to "I," but we reach
this end through a process of dialogue and not through
the dissection of an external object.

To the extent that conformity with the criteria of
science requires objective data obtained from outside
the dialogue, what is the status of psychoanalysis? In
the dialogue with persons one is never in the position
of putting nature to the question, when the observer
is a subject examining an outside object. For as soon
as we talk together we are not strange to one another;
we acquire one another's words and accordingly live
in one another's world. It is impossible for the as-
tronomer to do that with a star, or the geologist with
a rock, or even the physician with the patient's cardi-
ovascular system—except, in the last instance when
the heart comes into the question as a symbolic element. The rock and even the patient enter the observer's world as objects for some kind of manipulation. To be sure the patient in psychoanalysis is also
the object of manipulation, in that he seeks treatment
from another competent to produce change in him by
what he does; but the actions of the analyst, while
they intend a change, take place through an exchange.
Mind speaks for itself; everything else is spoken
about.

We have already seen in the preceding chapter that
Freud's early approach was that of the Hippocratic
physician. As soon as transference and countertrans-
ference entered into his thinking, he was working
from a radically different approach. The physician is
no longer outside the illness; he is part of it, to the
extent that he is the bearer of unconscious images
from the patient's past on the one side, and to the extent that he needs to be in tune with his own disposition to make the patient the bearer of unconscious images out of his own (the analyst's) past. Moreover, as
we shall see in greater detail, the arousal of personal,
historical images of one's own is not a handicap to the
analytic work unless it is neglected; on the contrary it
is an essential part of it. We only grasp the mental life
of another through the summoning up of these private
images out of our own past, but they become part of
the commonality of experience only when they pass
through the ordering, regulating and transforming system of language.

Freud's metapsychological theory, which is the
product of his attempt to make psychoanalysis a natural science without sacrificing its psychological base,
grew out of the position in which the dichotomy of
subject and object is taken for granted. The real is first
and foremost *res extensa*, the physical world known
through sense perception, and any other reality is constructed by analogy with physical reality. This does
not underestimate Freud's dedication to the concept
of psychic reality; far from it, for its strength lay for
him in its ready comparison with physical reality.

What prevailed in Freud's picture of psychic reality were descriptions and explanations that had their origins in the descriptions and explanations of physical reality, and for the good reason that they seemed to have behind them, for all the fluctuations of science, the solidity of the extended world that it was their purpose to describe and explain. The validity of physical science lies in the fact that its conclusions can be found to be false, but only by findings leading to other conclusions open to the same kind of verification. But can we ask questions about minds like the questions we can ask about the physical world?

Obviously we can if we intend to ask whether the action and integrity of mind depends on the action and the integrity of the brain. We also know that some are quite satisfied to know that. They must constitute a large proportion of the neuroanatomists and neurophysiologists, and of those psychologists and psychiatrists unaffected by psychoanalysis. But we apprehend the world, including the brain, in relation to the memories, conscious and unconscious, of all that has been our experience all our lives, an experience always lived in association with other lives. This is reality too.

To get a significant consequence of this idea we need only look again at the encounter of analyst and patient. Is it reducible or in any way translatable to an encounter between two brains? Manifestly not; in fact, we know about our own brains through no direct awareness either. I am not trying to solve the mind-body problem in stating that the reality of our being as we experience it precludes the possibility of reducing the psychic to the physical without remainder, except in death—and that reduction might stand for a definition of death. I can change the nature of psychic experience drastically through the use of psychotropic drugs, among other ways, but to do so, I must decide to do so, or someone else must make the decision for me to do it.

In the light of such or similar reflections we ask again, "Can we ask questions about the mind like those we ask about the physical world?" To do so is not merely to work with a global analogy: it is also to have to fit, stretch, cut, and fold our concepts of mind to make them adaptable to a physical grid. A careful analysis of Freud's metaphors in the writing of his early (and determinative) papers will show that this is just what took place (Morris, 1977). I realize that in all our considerations of mental processes we need to use metaphors drawn from physical states or acts, and my own verbs—"fit," "strength," "cut," "fold"—are examples; but there is a difference. When we speak or write metaphorically, as we do all the time, we borrow from the metaphor only those attributes immediately demonstrative of qualities we wish to show. In using his great neurological and physical analogues, Freud equipped his psychological concepts with properties fortifying to them—so long as we base psychoanalysis on the interpretive situation.

Even to speak of "mind" is to abstract from experience, and it is not surprising that there are languages, some within the Indo-European group, that have no word corresponding exactly to the English use of the word, perhaps because of its abstractness. What we mean by "mind" may be expressed by a variety of words that are not really synonymous with it or with one another: "experience," for example, or "thoughts," or "feeling," and in the most concrete sense "person." The primary attributes of "persons" do not belong to objects existing in space outside persons. Relevant ideas are "history," "anxiety," "experience," "language"—and maybe most definitive of all, "death," since persons while they are beings existing in time like all other beings, are aware of that existence and that it is of limited, if indefinitely limited, duration. Persons recall a past and project a future, and they engage in dialogues with one another that comprehend these expectations. All the events of persons are truly internalized; things do not just happen to them. Other beings exist for persons, either as other persons, or as things to use, contend with, or ignore, for example. No theory of human life can be true to its subject when it does not consider these things.

Looked at from the point of view of interpretation, psychoanalysis does in fact have at its center the existence of the person; all the neurobiological and other physicalist theorizing consists of an attempt to adapt the interpretive function of psychoanalysis to purposes foreign to its nature. Whether those purposes are necessary for an explanatory theory, as Ricoeur argues, or indeed whether an explanatory theory in the

intended sense of a theory of causal explanation is
necessary or desirable, is a question which we cannot
ignore. A lot depends on what else we have to offer.

Interpretation is inherent in speaking. Speaking is always explaining oneself (Palmer, 1969, chaps. 9–10).
Minimally, as command, for example, it is revealing
without further accounting a desire that is to be ful-
filled. Narrating, describing, planning are all interpretive. We do not select words all the time to fit them
to preexistent thoughts; that is something we do
either reflectively, critically, or with some intention
to impress or deceive that is conscious enough to
dominate the act of speaking. Ordinary statements are
the inner state they enunciate. Yet we often have the
feeling, at least on reflection, that we have not quite
said what we meant, and we cannot avoid the sense
that there is a ghost of meaning that does not get em-
bodied in words. This also is the "message" that is
supposed to be encoded and decoded, when both
speaker and hearer know the rules of communication
and abide by them. The question here is whether the
message does indeed have a wordless preexistence, as
pure image perhaps, just as the dream as it is dreamt
is wordless for the most part in its immediacy.

Mention of dreams reminds us that there is experience apart from words. The immense experience of
very early childhood is preverbal. It is not completely
unverbal to be sure, because parents are from the very
beginning designating events with words, and, maybe
of even greater importance, all of the categories of

daily events undergone by the infant are verbally prescribed: nursing is done along prescribed lines and so
are all the other procedures of infant care. The verbal
impinges on the preverbal at all times with the force
of a semiotic. Nevertheless there are experiences tied
primarily to images, and this preverbal disposition
persists throughout life. One of the unique achieve-
ments of psychoanalysis is effecting the passage from
imagining to speaking.[2]

It may be therefore that the sense of not having
said all we mean derives from the incomplete expres-
sibility in words of all that is imaginal in experience.
That this does not account for the phenomenon entirely is certain, since we may go on to state our further meaning later to more satisfaction. Ghosts of
meaning are probably like other ghosts, illusory; they
are in anticipatory form other statements belonging to
the mental events we are trying to announce. It is
quite true that in any instance we have not said all
that could be said; we cannot ever, even in the most
boringly obsessional monologues (perhaps least in
them), expose all the things sayable about anything.
But that does not leave us with an irreducible ineffable minimum. The tale is simply incomplete—always.

This insufficiency also has to do with the problem
of ambiguity. If no statement is fully complete, then

2. It will be evident that I am following here in my own fashion Lacan's theory of the relation of the "imaginary" (which I equate roughly
with "preverbal") and the "symbolic." (See Lacan 1977, chapters 1 and 3.)

any statement has more than one meaning. All statements, such as narrative accounts, are selective ren-
ditions, and one of the implicit meanings of them is
the basis of selection in the preconscious intention of
the speaker. No event is fully narrated: its being in
past time was other than the present rendition, as we
know from the testimony of other participants, but
what is said about the event, the rendition of the personal experience of it, is ambiguous because it is
framed in a language that has come from the general
community into the private experience of the speaker.
That is why speaking is inevitably interpretive, always explaining one's meaning.

In ordinary conversation, provided there is no reason for either speaker to be on guard against the de-
signs of the other, each interprets to the other as the
occasion arises for the further elucidation of meaning.
We assume that what each has to say is not the whole
story, but also that meaning will emerge more fully
with the submission of each to the questioning of the
other. But the dialogue is symmetrical, or when it is
not, as in the case of some conversations between
teacher and pupil, there is no expectation or need to
examine the medium of explanation. In ordinary conversation one asks the metalinguistic[3] question "What
do you mean by that?" without challenging the hon-
esty of the other, and "What I think you mean is
. . . " does not limit the possibility of demur. Expla-

3. "Whenever the addresser and/or the addressee need to check up
whether they use the same code, speech is focused on the CODE: it per-
forms a METALINGUAL (i.e. glossing) function" (Jakobson 1960, p. 356).

nations of that kind are further attempts at interpretation, at expansions of meaning.

There is another side to this. While I am a speaker interpreting my experience to my hearer, I am speaking to this hearer, not just anyone. My remarks are tailored to fit my knowledge of him or my expectations of him. This again is without conscious desire to impress or deceive. What is the apprehension of the hearer on which I depend in order to speak to him? We are familiar with the contrary case: the public figure whose conversation does not aim at this hearer, this unique person, but who has statements on all subjects that exist as if preformed and card catalogued, ready to be taken out. In such instances we may conclude that the speaker's expectations of his hearers are, if not zero, surely minimally distinguishable from his expectations of anyone else. The hearer is no one in particular. Since it may well be that most of the interlocutors of the speaker say the same things and ask the same questions, he is not entirely to be blamed. But this case is probably as far removed from the psychoanalytic situation as we can get, and it does not represent friendly colloquy either.

Ordinarily we engage in such friendly conversation for the purpose of gaining useful information or just because humans enjoy talking for its own sake. Speaker and listener (the roles being exactly reversible) are presented to one another in mutual recognition. He listens to me as I listen to him, and each act of listening is a self-imposed submission to the other (if "submission" is suspect, it is because we live in a

world that has exaggerated notions about independence). I need my listener and my listener needs me.
Also, and this is less evident, I have in my mind when
speaking to him a representation of him as listener. I
am not just hearing myself speak. It is a momentary
or longer identification with the listener. We have
overt experience of this when we say "I suppose you
think that this is . . . " We have at that moment put
ourselves in the position of the other, have become
the other, assumed his criticism and literally put it to
ourself. At the same time I must address not only this
hearer personally before me, and presumably known
to me, but also other persons associated with my
hearer in my own mind. Unlike the case of the public
personage mentioned, they are not just lay figures
who can stand for anyone at all; they are real persons—living or dead—with whom I have conversed in
the past or with whom I propose to speak in the future.

The upshot of this line of thinking is the realization that even the most ordinary conversation admits
the presence in imagination—conscious or unconscious—of more than the two actually visible in the
audible dialogue. In psychoanalytic terms, then, it is
clear that transference is a property of all dialogue, and
the only reason why that is not manifest is that it is
through psychoanalysis that we establish a setting for
the closest scrutiny of the dialogue.

Transference is not, however, simply one of many
constituents of dialogue with no special distinction. If

that were so it would not need a name of its own, nor could it occupy the central position in psychoanalysis that it does. What I have stated in this connection so far has been for the purpose of establishing the irreducible setting for transference to occur. It is possible only because we interpret ourselves through dialogue, and because we also present ourselves historically in dialogue. Neither of these is limited to psychoanalysis, but the asymmetry of the psychoanalytic dialogue, in which one of the participants is relatively silent, while the other not only speaks more, but agrees to speak freely without censorship, skews the dialogue. The thrust of the growing transference is backward: the other persons imaginally present arise from older and older currents of memory, and with them recur the long-forgotten desires against which the speaker has hitherto had to defend himself. On the analyst's side the interpretive action proceeds at once synchronically and diachronically. The present connections of the patient's utterances, including their deepest structures, are made plain, and their historical references are both defined and elucidated.

Transference is a misrecognition (Lacan, 1977, p. xi) of the other in the dialogue, more intensified perhaps than in ordinary conversation (although we never know this for sure since we do not usually analyze ordinary conversation), but it is not only a misrecognition. Transference is an expression of desire directed to the other of the dialogue. Is it a desire based on a misrecognition or a misrecognition based on a desire? Ricoeur, the most searching philosophical

critic of psychoanalysis, has contended that this discovery of Freud's, at least as early as *The Interpretation of Dreams*, put psychoanalysis in the way of de-
veloping as at once an interpretive, or hermeneutic
discipline, and an energetics, or economics. Once
Freud found that the dream, which we may look on as
the paradigm of utterances in psychoanalysis, is im-
pelled by the wish, the concept of force has entered
and cannot be denied. Granted such a claim, are we
not required to assent to the primacy of the energy
that drives the psychic processes?

I agree with Ricoeur that the concept of energetics
may be essential to an explanatory theory—if such a
theory needs to be modeled on the theories of natural
science. Freud thought that the facts of interpretive
experience forced such an explanation on him. The
motor of the dream is the unconscious wish, and such
wishes are displaceable. Accordingly they must have
some kind of generalized existence as part of a "reservoir of libido," to use one of Freud's telling analogies
(1923, pp. 63–66). As we have seen earlier, the re-
sounding trouble with the idea is that it moves us
from the human encounter to the impersonal explanation, and with the implication that pursued indefinitely, the impersonal explanation could exhaust the
meaning of the human encounter, a view which
seems to us to depart from reality.

Lacan has moved in the direction of solving this
problem by turning to structural linguistics. If laws of
the mind are to be found anywhere that conform to
the psychoanalytic situation of dialogue, where might

they better be found than in the laws of language? And
if man realizes himself through language (makes himself real), understanding language ought to be a way of
understanding man, in his unconscious as well as in
his conscious life. I shall in the next chapter make use
of some of the concepts of structural linguistics in my
analysis of interpretation, but I shall not go into them
further at this time. There is a more basic issue: how
are we to think theoretically at all about interpretation if we are not committed to a scientific determinism? For it does not make a great deal of difference in
our concept of man if we move from a biological to a
linguistic-structural determinism. For that matter the
two are possibly to be unified in a biogenetic structuralism, as Laughlin and d'Aquili (1974) have proposed.
Certainly in his own appropriation of structural linguistics to anthropology, Lévi-Strauss looks for mechanistic, deterministic laws to account for all cultural
forms.

I propose a kind of explanation that is not the same
as Freud's because it does not start with the axiom
(supposedly not an axiom but an observation from
analysis) that man's mental life is determined in a
way that is comparable to the deterministic explanations of natural science. Maybe it really is, but I shall
set the possibility aside. It seems to me that explanation in psychoanalysis, based entirely on the interpretation that grows out of the dialogue, is more like
something usually dismissed by the scientist as "mere
description." That is, we can narrate what happens in
a psychoanalytic session and can interpret the mean-

ings of the interchange. We can analyze our interpretations further through summaries and categorization, and we can continue this essentially descriptive process both intensively and extensively, not at any point neglecting the interpretation of desire, but also never departing from the principles of interpretation.

Clifford Geertz (1973, pp. 6–10) has used a term of Ryle's that might serve us as well in understanding what happens in psychoanalysis as it serves him in ethnography. The term is "thick description." It means explanation through as intensive as possible analysis of all the elements that go into a phenomenon. In ethnography it means "sorting out of the structures of signification and determining their social ground and import." Geertz compares the process with "trying to read (in the sense of 'construct a reading of') a manuscript—foreign, faded, full of ellipses, but written not in conventionalized graphs of sound but in transient examples of shaped behavior." He further says: "Anthropological writings are interpretations, which means that they are fictions in the sense that they are 'something made'; 'something fashioned'—the original meaning of *fictio*–not that they are false, unfactual or merely 'as if' experiments. Through them the scientific imagination gets into touch with the lives of strangers" (p. 15).

Psychoanalytic theory can be likened to ethnography, in that it also aims at "sorting out the structures of signification"; in the case of psychoanalysis the "ground" of these structures is personal and historical, and only secondarily social. As with ethnography, meanings progress into greater abstraction from the experiences narrated and inferred with the goal of conceptualization, but the concepts formed are always descriptive summaries and inferences. They are a far cry from anything that can be tested in any imaginable kind of laboratory. "What kind of laboratory is it," Geertz asks, "where *none* of the parameters are manipulable?" (p. 22). The purpose of the theory is rather "to ferret out the unapparent import of things" (p. 26). In this way "thick description" differs from observational scientific theory in the relative modesty of its application; but unlike observational scientific theory it is concerned with the immediate data of human experience, and it makes up in interest and importance for what it lacks in exactitude on the one hand and generalizability on the other.

I am of course aware of the profound contradiction existing between Geertz's point of view and that of Lévi-Strauss. The latter is the ethnographer who does not himself venture into the field of study, but who establishes high-level constructions on the basis of his reading of other ethnographers' writings. These constructions designate for him determining forces equivalent to the energetics of traditional Freudianism, and he has assembled all-inclusive theories with respect to kinship and myth, for example. To follow Geertz on the other hand, applying his idea to psychoanalysis, would end up by our restricting our generalizations about the structure of the unconscious to a small number of categories—or at least smaller than our present stock—and they would keep much closer to the clinical scene than our most prominent theorists have. At all events, we work in a different field, in which the "reporters" are there before us for a long while, so that we can continue to confront them with their inconsistencies and their doubts, and we do not know how far we might go with our jointly constructed "fictions" toward the elegance of theory. It must be a different kind of theory from what we have known, but not one that ignores or misrepresents the intentional nature of the unconscious.

Let us explore this a bit further. It is latent intention that we discover when we analyze, and the participation of any intention in an endless (but not formless) network of latent intentions. The network has a temporal dimension, and in fact we have seen that its temporality is of its essence. We must be able, using any theory of psychoanalysis that will stand, to tell the history of this network of latent intentions on the basis of the psychoanalytic process as it grows out of the psychoanalytic dialogue. This amounts to substituting a historical explanation for the naturalistic explanation of Freud's energetics; it is also a historical explanation based on the elucidation of contemporaneous latent intentions. We shall at another point look into the ways in which the past is recovered in psychoanalysis, but it is manifestly true—as long as we keep in mind the method of the psychoanalytic dialogue, from which all literal documentation is strictly absent—that we move from synchronic description to diachronic description, all the while testing and enriching the categories of our interpretations.

As an example consider such a category of interpretation as sadomasochism. We know that the concept was adapted by Freud, from its original uses to
designate certain special forms of sexual enjoyment.
Freud discovered that unconsciously these opposites
stand in complementary or even contrapuntal relation
to one another. Like others of Freud's central concepts,
such as the Oedipus complex and narcissism, the
vivid imagery of the term affects observations that
become categorically adherent to it, but the adven-
tures of the Marquis de Sade, and the novels of Sacher-
Masoch do not make the terms derived from their
names less suitable to designate implicit metaphoric
and metonymic relations in patients' narratives. Sado-
masochism, once we are made aware of it as a possibility in the derived senses to which Freud has extended it, stands out in a patient's associations to the
point where we can recognize it in his or her present
life, past desires, and expectations in the transference.
Granted that we retain that spirit of skeptical inquiry
without which we are blinded by one insight and see
no more thereafter, we can accord to sado-masochism
the significances it deserves in this patient as a fundamental network of intentions. We can reconstruct
its larval forms in earlier periods of his history, and we
can relate it to the experience the patient has had. The
deeper the analysis, the more intricate—the "thicker"—
the description.

We do not reach by this route the kind of causal
explanation possible in physical science. It is more
like the causality of history, which also consists of the

causality of past intentions.[4] How much of the present conceptual structure of psychoanalysis can be preserved following this route is uncertain to me. If, for example, we try to show how sado-masochism and narcissism are related, all that we can do is to point to the history of the interrelations of such intentions in a patient or in a summary account of many patients. We shall get out of it a history of desire—a "natural history" perhaps, but only in the sense that we can generalize for human experience clusters of intentions determined by the fact of being human in the human world, and in this particular life.

What happens to anxiety, which has been theoreti-

4. Here I refer the reader to R. Collingwood (1975, pp. 214–15) who contrasts physical and historical explanations thus:

> For science, the event is discovered by perceiving it, and the further search for its cause is conducted by assigning it to its class and determining the relation between that class and others. For history, the object to be discovered is not the mere event, but the thought expressed in it. To discover that thought is already to understand it. After the historian has ascertained the facts there is no other process of inquiring into their causes. When he knows what happened, he already knows why it happened. . . . The processes of nature can therefore be properly described as sequences of mere events, but those of history cannot. They are not processes of mere events but processes of actions, which have an inner side, consisting of processes of thought. . . . All history is the history of thought.

With proper adjustment, these reflections aptly define the contrast between natural science and psychoanalytic science, too. We are required to understand the word "unconscious" wherever we read the word "thought" (although by no means excluding conscious thoughts in so doing), but in general the distinction stands. I shall differentiate between history in Collingwood's sense and the personal history in which psychoanalysis is interested in chapter 4.

cally implicated with psychoanalytic explanation from the beginning? Freud's (1926, p. 92) own move from the first to the second anxiety theory is highly suggestive. The first theory is rooted in his oldest biological conceptions: anxiety is a libido that has undergone a quasi-chemical degradation. Here causality reigns; the evidently physiological quality of anxiety (as of all other emotions) dominates the explanation, even though no directly physical agencies are implied in it. With the concept of *signal* anxiety we stand on a different ground: the word itself is promising. Now the explanation—on which the whole theory of defense is erected—is made in terms of meaning. An event has occurred, and an experience is coming to be, which is interpreted as a danger; an affective-cognitive change takes place. With this second anxiety theory we use once more the language of interpretive description. That the signal is given regularly, that there are regularities of defense is only a higher order of description. We do nothing to exclude the psychosomatic unity, but we do deny that psychoanalysis has anything to tell us about the physiological chemistry of anxiety and the other emotions, only about the "signals" and "signs" from which their meaning and history are interpretable.

I cannot see how we could proceed from here to hang on to a theory of instincts, as generalizations. Human desires may indeed be classified according to their libidinal and destructive intentions, but once we postulate a libidinal instinct, for example, as something superordinately anterior or prior to the experiences recalled or reconstructed in analysis, we have departed from any continuous sequence of historical interpretations and are borrowing an idea that is empty of psychoanalytic meaning.[5]

Nor are we any better off with many of the notions of ego psychology of the more recent past. Ideas like "neutralization," "autonomous ego sphere," or "adaptive functions of the ego" are all rational concepts accounting after the fact for something that happened.[6] They are not derivable from the psychoanalytic dialogue, and indeed they sometimes are used like the *ex post facto* explanations of changes in the stock mar-

5. Kohut (1959, pp. 477–78) in an important article, "Introspection, Empathy and Psychoanalysis," anticipates some aspects of my point of view, although without reference to the dialectical operations of psychoanalysis. For Kohut, the observational data of psychoanalysis are the reported introspections of the patient, as well as those of the analyst, and the latter's capacity to know empathically the unuttered introspections of the patient. These psychological observations are for him, as for me, the substance of the whole procedure and "it is erroneous to extrapolate the interpretation of a specific mental state from biological principles, especially if they contradict our psychological findings." Further, "the final psychological proof for the factual existence [of unconscious longings of any sort] must be in their introspective and empathic discovery." Kohut maintains further that "much clarity is gained if we admit that the psychoanalytic term 'drive' is derived from the introspective investigation of inner experience." I believe that this admission comes down to recognizing that "drive" like "instinct" in the psychoanalytic sense is at most a useful summarizing description.

6. The quoted comments originated, or course, with Heinz Hartmann. My skepticism about their usefulness, or even relevance, to psychoanalytic theory does not extend to the larger work of this powerful thinker. Like Kris's famous phrase cited in connection with them, they have by currency become clichés, obstacles to thought, and therefore no credit to their creators.

ket. They may help to promote an agreeable sense of closure in the mind of the analyst, and to the extent that this is desirable they may have some therapeutic usefulness. And Ernst Kris's contribution to psychoanalysis would not be unappreciated if no one ever referred again to "regression in the service of the ego," that now exhausted slogan purporting to explain the appearance of creativity where symptoms might have been expected.

Someone, possibly a physician, will ask what is curative about a psychoanalytic theory that is wholly based on interpretation? It was so much easier to account for the therapeutic effect of psychoanalysis when we could follow Freud's libido theory and see in the lifting of repression the release of energy, hitherto bound by the defensive agency of the ego, now available for the ego's work in the real world (Freud, 1917, p. 454). And indeed if anyone wants that kind of explanation I can see no reason why he should not have it and still analyze properly, since such explanations rarely influence one's practice. Our alternative is not the same thing in different words, however, because it stems from another concept of what psychoanalysis is all about. It explains less, but it means more, when we say that the curative factor of the psychoanalytic dialogue is to be found in greater and deeper self-knowledge, realizing more and more who this is living this life in this world, and especially the new knowledge of one's own desire.

3

Interpretation and the Interpreter

Confronted by the unfamiliar or the unforeseen, we marvel, and then we interpret. An exotic scene, a strange religious rite, above all and most commonly a foreign language in a situation in which we cannot evade a demand made on us provides such a confrontation. Marveling is not a human prerogative alone: even my dog marvels when she sees a garbage bag at night and by her behavior appears to mistake it for the neighbor's cat. But only humans, and a few selected anthropoids trained to use their latent potentials, move from marveling to interpreting. In fact our human marveling is itself not free from interpreting: when we wonder, we wonder *what*? We implicate in our wonderment a surmise linking the novelty with things already known. Unlike the dog, we do not necessarily make the linkage dogmatically; for us wondering is questioning, at least when we are in our best form, and we do not go into action without conjecture.

Interpretation of this kind has no assurance of being correct, no assurance, that is, that the logical ordering we make on encountering a novelty will cor-

respond with the logic of its own nature. At far re-
move from the ordinary, take for example Schiapa-
relli's Martian "canals," which for so long seemed to
some astronomers to be evidence of human intelligence on Mars. Linear streaks were visible, and were
neutrally named *canali*; the erroneous translation of
the Italian word into the English "canals" instead of
"channels" implied intelligent making. It was a mis-
interpretation in two steps, since further and closer
inspection revealed that the lines are neither canals
nor channels.

The error of Martian canals teaches us that any
classification of the unknown seems better than none.
We are intolerant of marvels; everything needs to be
subsumed into the ordinary or we are made anxious.
The genius that makes something new does so first by
withholding judgment in interpreting. At our best we
follow wonder with a certain suspension, awaiting
more information before deciding. What we do decide
on immediately, unless we are too dazzled by the marvel, is that what we have observed is to be a sign for
us of something. As a sign it exists in and of itself, but
also in the place of something else, which is to be defined at greater leisure. Interpretation is the reading of
signs.

Traditionally this is the work of the soothsayer,
the astrologer, the magician, the witchdoctor, and
shaman. It is also the property of all men and women
noted for their "wisdom" in the popular meaning of
that word. They know when the weather is due for a
change, and what kind of crop there will be, when the

fever will break; they can detect signs of a child's later character in present traits as they can foresee from the lines in the palm the outlines of destiny to be revealed in the distant sequel. Signs also—as in the New Testament—are equivocal demonstrations of the divine presence, evident as such only to the elect; otherwise they are mute, being comprehended only literally.

To be sure, we can think of signs along these lines without recourse to such mysteries. Something may be a sign of something just because we know from past experience that when "a" happens, "b" follows. This kind of sign, called signal, cannot be recognized when what confronts us is really new, because its efficacy as signal requires past experience. We can all the same, usually by analogizing, make the inference that if something like "a" happens, "b" or something like "b" will follow (not necessarily in temporal sequence, but in the order of our recognition). The most familiar examples of signs as signals are road signs, such as those in which the contours of the road that are being approached are depicted by lines we can recognize as the usual conventions for such contours, wavy lines for curves, etc. The literally blatant signal is the car horn, and for some this is the only proper use of the term signal, since it includes the necessary temporality of this kind of sign: "b" must follow "a" in time.

I shall not take up the theory of signs in detail, but I shall make reference to its constituents from time to time, because, as we have anticipated in tracing the development of the theory of psychoanalytic interpretation, a theory of signs has gradually grown out of—and into—psychoanalytic theory itself. Here let me simply state that the most general meaning of interpretation rests on a theory of signs, for example, that the presence of something implies the presence of something else. The two main lines of progress of the theory of signs have been the philosophical and the linguistic, which have naturally often crossed; only in recent years have they moved openly into psychoanalytic theory. Charles S. Peirce (1839–1914) opened the way through his classification of the sign as (1) icon, which is a likeness used as a sign (such as a pencil streak representing a geometrical line, which itself has no objective existence); (2) index, which has a physical connection with an object but no likeness to it (such as Thoreau's famous "circumstantial evidence" in the shape of a milk bottle with a trout inside it) and which psychologically, according to Peirce, "depends upon association by contiguity"; and (3) symbol, comprising "all words, sentences, books and other conventional signs." Peirce insisted that the symbol as word is purely a convention (in Saussure's term, it is "arbitrary"), even etymologically; the word stands for an idea, not for a "real object" [Buchler, 1955, chap. 7].

The theory of signs was stated within linguistics by F. de Saussure, who distinguished between the "signifier" and the "signified." The fundamental matter for us is that Saussure and Peirce both refuted the general empiricist assumption that the word as sign is simply the name for a thing. On the contrary, the word designates a thought or concept, not a percept. The importance of this distinction can be recognized when we reflect on the fact that our whole ordering of the world of things is a conceptual structure, so that the real world takes on for us values given in the structure of our language.

The peculiarity of words as signs is that unlike other signs, we do not immediately recognize them as such. We treat them as though they formed a perspicuous and identity-less medium through which something substantive and substantial is transmitted. We know better than this all the time, but limit our knowledge of the contrary to the instances of exceptions to ordinary communication. Poetic expression is one form of verbal use that we can, as a rule, recognize as having the sign function: in reading or saying the poem we dwell on the words themselves instead of seeing "through" them into a meaning that we can conceive as existing apart from them. Of course, real objects and actions and the relations among them exist apart from words, but meaning does not, whether in poetry, prose, or ordinary speech. When we wish to convey an idea we can do so only by stating it in words and sentences. If the statement displeases us, or if it fails to communicate our meaning, we try again in other words, hoping that this time our meaning will be conveyed. "Hitting upon" the right words is to utter (at least to ourselves, not necessarily aloud) a meaning. We have the feeling all the same that this meaning exists as a something else that we "put into words," and I believe that this feeling, whether it is appropriate or not, requires further discussion, which I shall undertake at a later point.

At the same time that it is in and through words that all meaning is conveyed, we note two other things: one is that as Peirce first put it, "the word itself has no existence" but "existents will conform to it" (Buchler, 1955, p. 112), and second, that expressing the primacy of the word does not exclude the possibility of meaningful wordless actions. In the first comment, we point to the division of the word as sign into signifier and signified—here using Saussure's (1966) terms. The word, which when spoken is a physical acoustic entity that can be written down with an ordinary writing instrument or recorded as vibrations of a stylus, and that can be classified phonetically and semantically (as "signifier"), is also purely arbitrary and yet at the same time, according to Benveniste, uniquely fits a specific ideational concept.[1] "Cow," which is a sound in the English language having in itself no special kinship with the animal so designated, also is uniquely associated with the idea (the "signified") that we have of that animal. The second comment, of lesser moment, merely is to remind us that we perform all sorts of actions silently and without conscious inner speech (Mahl, 1967); to assume that such actions could exist in the absence of language of some sort is, however, mistaken, since learn-

---

1. Benveniste's point (1966) is that within the language the relation between signifier and signified is not arbitrary; on the contrary, it is necessary. It is possible to think of something only through the use of the word assigned to it.

ing to perform them depends on the presence of the ability to speak if not in the pupil, then at least in the teacher.

It is not far from these linguistic considerations to the view that all speaking is interpretation of some sort. That is, we cannot use the "medium" of meaning without telling what we mean. To speak at all is to locate meaning in the "house" of language, to borrow Heidegger's striking expression (Palmer, 1969, p. 135). If this is so for speaking (by which we mean here writing as well) of "objective" matters, it is all the more certainly so for personal discourse of the sort engaged in during psychoanalysis. I am literally interpreting my experience when I tell it. My world becomes words, and not only words, but sentences and longer utterances, because my world is lived in language from the beginnings of my postnatal life, although at the very beginning all the language is that of others. The experiences narrated exist in the narration, first, and then in the narrative, which having been uttered has an existence for me and for my listener—as much in the absence as in the presence of recording. We shall also see how all we can hope to recover of the past in psychoanalysis hangs from the unity of experience and language.

Although this first order of interpretation is not what we are concerned with in psychoanalysis, I do not think we can rightly understand psychoanalytic interpretation without seeing on what it is based. The medium is not autonomous, neither for the narrator nor for the listener, who in the psychoanalytic setting becomes the interpreter of the second order; or better, one of the two such, since his patient is also one. The meanings, unconscious meanings, which are the special domain of psychoanalysis, are based on the consciously intended meanings or interpretations that appear in the utterances of both patient and analyst.

No one goes about speaking by deliberately choosing all or even most of his words, although we sometimes say that we do. Choosing our words is an alteration of them, expressing a different experience from the one manifested in the unaltered state. We feel this whenever we try to speak a language in which we are not perfectly fluent; then we choose our words, not necessarily by translating, like a beginner in the language, but by a conscious striving after the right word. The native speaker, or the perfectly fluent foreigner is not aware of any difference between the words he is speaking and the ideas and experiences that he intends to speak. There is no veil, and the words seem not to exist because they have perfect transparency, which is the business of psychoanalysis to diminish. Whenever the analyst confronts the patient with a word or phrase just uttered, he points to the masking, screening property of language. By this intervention he aims to expose the nonrational, nonlogical intention that the word or phrase seems to hint at in the context at hand. It is no doubt the perfection of language as a medium that so long delayed its being subjected to scientific study. It was easy to use language to talk about everything in nature outside language, but much more difficult to take language as its own object of discourse; correspondingly, no doubt, that also accounts for the priority of diachronic linguistics, the study of language change and distribution, over synchronic linguistics, the study of language as it exists in the present.

"Psychoanalysis is interpretation from beginning to end," as we have already cited Paul Ricoeur[2] and I do not see how anyone can contest that so long as we are discussing psychoanalysis as a praxis, a method, a process. It is more difficult to defend the statement if it defines psychoanalysis as a science, even apart from any claims to be akin to the physical sciences. We shall try to see whether Ricoeur's description holds for the science too, but it is enough for the moment to take it in its more limited application. It states, in effect, that psychoanalysis is a reading of signs. How does this reading take place?

It was no accident that it began in a physician's consulting room. We have discussed its historical antecedents earlier. The sign and the symptom are the physician's introduction to the patient, or, rather, the symptom motivates the patient to approach the physician, and the physician looks for the sign. Here perhaps is interpretation at its most naive, by which I do not mean simple. A painful sensation or a physical limitation can call for relief, first of all, and for diag-

2. Hans Loewald (1971) among others has also insisted on this, but within the general context of metapsychology. While metapsychology may begin in interpretation, it claims to go beyond description, even the "thick description" I have alluded to in chapter 2, to an explanation in terms of a world outside the intersubjective situation.

nosis secondarily. The symptom is a sign for the patient only to the extent of his fear of what it might betoken; for the physician the symptom is primarily important because of its function as a sign of disease. In a way the symptom is the ideal sign, because it is something real enough in itself, as the sufferer well knows, yet its interpretation reveals something else.

To begin with there was no clear distinction between the symptom of physical disorder and the symptom of neurosis. Accordingly the first and most thoroughly explored neurotic experience in psychoanalysis was hysteria, in which the physical symptom was paramount (whether it still is, is not so sure).[3] If a physical symptom did not yield to the appropriate remedies, and its interpetation as a sign of underlying disease proved incorrect, then it was to be assumed that it was a sign of something else. Freud's great insight was that the symptom was a sign that had meaning.

If all discourse is interpretive in the meaning here advanced, what distinguishes psychoanalytic discourse? Technical rules are indispensable to the method, and they are mainly rules constraining the discourse within certain rather narrow limits. Psy-

3. It remains an unsolved mystery whether hysterical symptoms have changed and possibly even declined in frequency in any forms since Freud's classical studies were published, or whether they are only diagnosed differently. Thus, Ilza Veith (1965) concluded her historical study of hysteria with these words: " . . . it may not be too paradoxical to state that it was the intensified understanding of the cause of hysteria by leading psychiatrists during this century that contributed to the near-disappearance of the disease."

choanalytic discourse is not supposed to resemble ordinary conversation very much, and still less is it like
a lecture addressed by an expert to a learning audi-
ence. On the contrary, the major burden of speaking is
thrust upon the patient, and one might understand the
situation as a very sophisticated variety of medical
consultation, in which the patient brings his narrative
to the physician as the object of a scientific scrutiny,
which is to result in the application of remedial words
to it. It is not an entirely erroneous view, and it grows
naturally enough out of the medical milieu in which
psychoanalysis came to be. What such a view leaves
out is the dialogue. It moves in the direction dear to
the modern scientist, toward the computerized management of illness, in which the therapeutic action is
taken by an instrument free of human passions and
therefore of human blind spots, as well as incapable of
a participating response. Such a person or such a computer indisputably could do something that cannot be
done in dialogue, because he, she, or it could be pro-
grammed to be attuned to many signs and never be
misled by their contradictory nature, as the practi-
tioner can. What is lacking in the picture is the life of
the "observer," and maybe most lacking of all is the
life of the imagination.

What the "objective" model of the interpreter envisages is someone free of presuppositions, prejudices,
preconceptions about the person before the interpreter, unmoved by immediate emotional reactions,
and unaffected also by a personal history. Ideally such
an observer would not even know anything about psy-

choanalysis as a theory, so that his mind could not be made up in advance; he would be in no danger of merely sliding his observations into the appropriate slots. His language would be colorless, pellucid, incapable of discouragement for the patient as it would be incapable of seductiveness. But enough of such a fantasy, worthy of being mentioned only because the hankering after its realization persists in some quarters, if not explicitly then in a scientific disguise. And no wonder, when scientific medicine, which always treats men and women as objects has had such brilliant, life-saving successes. A double-blind research method is bound to be a desideratum wherever illness (including mental illness) is in question. At present we see such an attempt to objectify psychoanalysis in the recorded transcription of psychoanalysis. It is presumed in this research that the introduction of equipment and prospective listeners can be written off as a constant variable. It is apparently not necessary to remember that Freudian psychoanalysis in its entirety has been formulated in the absence of witnesses to the dialogue.

The psychoanalyst cannot be blind. He cannot enter the field without presuppositions. He cannot be without a personal history. His language, as much as his patient's, speaks his history and no other's, and as a system of signs, it bears the marks of his most private existence. In fact that is a reason for one of the most generally accepted technical rules—the relative silence of the analyst. Yet while he can be verbally silent and control his expression and gestures, or at least not demonstrate them to his patient, with the assistance of special arrangements (the couch), he cannot be inwardly silenced. His history organized the life he is now living with his patient. That is quite a different situation from the surgeon's, for whom the signs are rarely discovered in discourse with the patient, and even when they are, derive their usefulness more from the ordinariness of language than from those redundant elements that literally characterize the individuality of the patient in analysis.

I have wondered at times what it would be like if we could find someone totally ignorant of psychoanalysis as method or theory, but in other respects an educated man or woman, and train such a person in the psychoanalytic method of listening and in a psychoanalytic recognition of the meaning of signs. This would be as close as we could get to a presuppositionless psychoanalyst, someone who would not be already equipped with the set of categorical divisions that we employ as we sift out the structures that we believe we have discovered through psychoanalytic discourse and have confirmed through objective and developmental studies. Would this hypothetical observer rediscover the great Freudian categories? Even raising the question—and here there is no idea of the affectless, history-less computer-analyst—betrays an unrealistic view: it is impossible for an educated modern person of the western world to be ignorant of the Freudian categories. A Kaspar Hauser would not be educable as a psychoanalyst precisely because he would have fallen into the world from a sphere, or risen from a cellar, outside history. On the other hand there have been enough defections from psychoanalysis for us to know that some of the defectors have tried our system and found it wanting. Whether it was the system as an interpretive method that they found wanting is not so clear; to study psychoanalysis has also entailed a great deal more, namely a metapsychology that has achieved the same rank as the interpretive method, or even a higher one.

But the reason for trying to conceive of the presuppositionless psychoanalyst was really quite different. I meant to cast into contrast the situation as it actually exists. The real analyst comes to the analysis of patients under the influence of a very large amount of psychoanalytic theory. It is to be assumed that he has personally verified the theory, as far as anyone can, learning from his own experience as patient the discernible constants in mental processes as derivable from the discourse. He has expectations drawn from his knowledge of his own world about what is likely to be in his patient's world. Whatever his views on the Oedipus complex for example, he will expect evidences of its presence or its equally significant absence; even its absence will be contingent on the theoretical position that "it" (a definable constellation of intrafamilial experiences) has been prevented—rather than the idea that its absence contradicts Freud's theory. A reading of the transference is, generally speaking, a reading of the Oedipus complex and its deficiencies and transformations. We enter the psychoanalytic situation not as if it were a fresh encounter—to which we bring nothing but our human experience, such wisdom as we may have acquired through living, our moral principles, and a desire to be of help—but with a theoretical position about human nature which establishes the horizons within which we will interpret the language of the patient. Our justification for doing so is that the theory—or at least those aspects of it to which we adhere—has been sufficiently confirmed; we will test the theory in respect to its dependent hypotheses, but we will not have to go outside the theory as a whole. If, as has happened rather remarkably of late under the influence of the attack on the theory of penis envy in women, we come to see that some aspects of the theory were incorrect, the error being due, as in this instance, to unexamined social prejudices, we have recourse to other aspects of the theory to make the experiences intelligible.

The great hinge on which the whole enterprise swings is the concept of the unconscious. As we have already seen, the unconscious was conceived without the aid of linguistic knowledge, and yet not so far from it either. The idea, drawn really from the contemporary theory of hypnosis, that what is unconscious is "counter will" (Breuer and Freud, 1893, p. 5) implies that what is unconscious seeks expression, being a "will," and that puts the unconscious into the realm of discourse. However conceived, the unconscious is not proved anew in every psychoanalysis; it is the concept that governs the analyzing process. We have only once again to contrast psychoanalytic discourse

with ordinary conversation to see how this is. In ordinary dialogue interpretations take place as one
speaker constructs his own thought by making it
known, and reconstructs the thought of the other by
making the other's utterances also his own. The interpretations are bilateral and mutual, but while the two
may think they have reason to be suspicious or skeptical of one another, they do not scan one another's
utterances for signs of the "will" contrary to the
manifest one. Psychoanalytic procedure necessitates
this kind of scanning; it takes place in a unique way,
not under the domination of suspicion, but, on the
contrary, facilitated by a suspension of even normal
mistrust. Preliminary to scanning, however, is the implicit recognition that it will yield results: we "know"
in advance that this kind of examination of the discourse will demonstrate ideas and intentions to which
ordinary conversation is opaque.

I do not think that this point requires fuller illustration. Crude criticisms of psychoanalysis have been
made from time to time, disposed to contest its validity by showing from case histories that interpretations vary with theoretical preconceptions. If we have
any grasp of the idea of the sign, it would be a wonder
if they did not. The linguistic sign exists only in a
world of language; it has no privacy but that of the
world in which it occurs. If the presuppositions with
which I enter the analytic dialogue as analyst (here in
the most general sense of the word) do not include the
focal concept of the Oedipus complex, but instead,
say, the concept of archetypal figures superordinate to

the personal family, then it is to be expected that the signs will be read accordingly. There is to be sure a problem of truth here, and that requires careful attention.

Meanwhile, let us return to the consulting room of the Freudian psychoanalyst. Beyond his theoretical and technical equipment, he is still less to be thought of as without presuppositions when we reflect on him as a person. It is interesting that a certain facelessness has come to be the mark of the analyst, or, at any rate, the analyst at work: the penetrating gaze, the impassive face, the deliberate speech, the unrevealing surroundings—nothing to impose upon the fantasy of the patients and nothing to limit the freedom of its range. For good or bad that is the outward setting in many instances. The analyst as person, the interpreter to others, is also the interpreter to himself. He listens and speaks from a world in which he alone is native, even though it is also a world shared with others. It is from this world, this life, this history, that he joins in an exploration of another world, life, history.

Psychoanalytic method is a technique, a designed way of going about analyzing and interpreting. It is an artifice, not a natural interchange that grows inevitably out of the human situation. Man exists in language, which is to say in conversation, which may also be artificial, through the adoption of a formal manner or through the intended limitation of what is to be discussed. A seminar is an artificial conversation too. Psychoanalysis is also not what it has been thought sometimes to be, a process of objective examination. The analyst is not, in principle, like a surgeon laying bare a mental region and treating it as an object for his subjective appraisal, although in actual practice he does that at certain times. It is this anomalous position of psychoanalysis with respect to the interchange between analyst and patient that calls its authenticity into question. For being neither natural conversation, nor the deliberate formal interchange of the seminar, nor an objective appraisal of data, what is it?

An objective technique would be something like this: One would work with a historical text, as though the text were a thing like another mute thing. The comparison above with surgical procedure is inadequate, because the surgeon knows all the time that the object of his investigation and operation is a living, feeling, thinking person, hoping for cure and fearful of death. More apposite would be the examination of a specimen from inanimate nature or from animate nature considered only in its objective aspects. A text can be so considered when, for example, it is examined for inconsistencies of spelling or when it is compared with another text of the same work in search of alterations made by the author. This is strictly noninterpretive text criticism, which changes when someone begins to inquire about the meaning of the alterations. Then the critic puts the text to the question, confronts the text as though it could speak to him, attempting to satisfy himself that the explanation that he offers for the alterations cannot be falsified by reference to the text or to some other text which has relevance to the first. Even in the instance when interpretation of this sort takes place, it is quite different from the kind of interpretation with which we are concerned. The questions, to be sure, arise in the same way, from the spontaneous interest of the prepared interpreter, but they are framed within the narrow limits of this investigation. I know that I cannot expect to find any answer in a given text to questions which relate to a historical event that has taken place after the composition of the text. Moreover, although I must have a prepared mind and cannot approach a text of any sort critically without suitable education, the line between the content of the text and my personal life and its preferences, while never an absolute division, is at least to some extent definable. The more my own world—which is far more extensive than my professional or literary or historical competence—intrudes on my observation of the text, the less likely am I to remain faithful to the work before me. Exceptions to this rule may come, maybe more in the work of the most gifted than in others, but they only illuminate the truth of the rule by their rarity.

Naturally, the further removed the critic is from this kind of approach to his text, the nearer he may be to a psychoanalytic position. When he enters into a dialogue with the text, he is allowing himself to pay attention to the appeal of the writing to him, as though it had been written for him, were addressed to him. This is also the way of the good reader, whether his reading be fiction or of a work in a sacred tradition.

Depending on the vitality of the critical powers that still attend our reading, we shall be more or less likely to read to some purpose. There is always the danger that entering into a dialogue with a text, not intended directly for us, we shall be carried into fantastic extremes of private or ad hoc interpretation. The history of the reading of the Bible is strewn with examples. Committed passionately to a special fiction about the text, one proves the fiction over and over again.

Psychoanalytic listening, with the famous "evenly suspended attention" recommended by Freud, is a deliberately designed undertaking. It is more often than not learned by example, so that styles of listening are transmitted from analysts to their patients in training. The transmission is not always literal; the patient in training analysis may indeed closely imitate his analyst's manner, but he may also exaggerate its features, or caricature or reverse them. At all events, while we may teach the method in lecture and seminar, it is far from a simple rule to be applied in all cases.

How is attention evenly suspended? I am as listener supposed to be able to open my mind to the discourse of the person before me. That he or she is lying on a couch and is not facing me does not always facilitate this. It is easier for the mind to wander into private channels when no one is physically confronting the listener. One depends on a commitment to the patient, which is no more and no less than any other commitment, to ensure that one's attention is directed to him and not to oneself, except in so far as private reflection has a bearing on the discourse of the

patient. It is impossible to exaggerate the importance
of this point, since it gives an indication of the vari-
ability of the setting in which analysis takes place. It
is a gross falsification that puts the listening analyst
in the position of the kind of scientific observer who
is simply open to the facts before him, allowing them
to test the validity of his hypothesis. Even though we
add to the "facts" under observation the ramifications
of private thought, we unduly objectify the nature of
the work. The observer is part of the observed; the
subject–object dichotomy is blurred from the outset.

What appears to govern attention so that it has
some purpose, and does not float so freely that it settles nowhere, is the attraction of the unexpected.
Interpretation, I have said, begins in marveling. The
psychoanalytic listener is peculiarly attuned to the
lesser orders of marvel. A slip of the tongue is only an
extreme example of what I mean, far less important
than a subtly striking allusion or an association of ordinarily unrelated ideas. Learning to hear such connections is like learning any other primarily aesthetic
skill, the relations of colors or of tones, for example,
which requires a long schooling of submission to
sense experience. Yet this is not intuitive in the loose
sense of that word, not at all. The attention settles
when it grasps something quite concrete, which is
often, if not always, a recognized figure of speech, or
trope.

What sort of figures command our attention? In a
sense it is anything that is redundant with respect to
factual communication, anything that could be easily

omitted in a telegraphic statement or in a prepared summary. Significance therefore is to be found exactly where it is ordinarily not found: in the seemingly decorative, amplifying, embellishing, explicative detail. Such words might suggest incorrectly that the speaker needs to have some literary or rhetorical command over language that is the prerogative of the specialist. Not at all, as Montaigne wrote; everyone, including "vostre chambrière" speaks in tropes. Uneducated language uses just as colorful figures as educated, but they are likely to be fewer, more repetitious, and less personal. Nor is it necessarily the more vivid allusion that engages our attention. "I think I shall wear my black dress," the patient says (or used to say). "Why black?" is the question instantly aroused in the analyst's mind, with the accompanying chorus of personal allusions—mourning, formality, self-discipline, or understated self-display.

It would probably not be possible to make an exhaustive catalogue of the types of trope that arouse the questioning of the analytic listener, not that there are so many, but because many of them would fall between categories. Parallelisms, repetitions, ambiguities, both syntactical and lexical, metaphor, metonymy and synecdoche make up a good number of them. Of them, metaphor stands out, as Lacan has shown on many occasions, for the reason that it is the representative figure of all language. Language is always metaphoric in the sense that the word is always substitutive for the absent thing. When therefore we hear a metaphor in the usual sense of that word, we are struck by it, because it is language analyzing itself. Hearing, or even just suspecting, the metaphor, we ask "What is hidden there?" What Freud first exposed in the "psychopathology of everyday life," in the psychology of slips and errors understood as symptoms, is now revealed in the common figures of speech. Psychoanalysis treats all figures of speech after the manner of treating symptoms—but also all symptoms after the manner of treating figures of speech.

Such rhetorical evidences of hidden ideas are not always so strikingly given. To be sure it is the vivid turn of phrase that of itself attracts our attention, but even that may be only a signal that something else, more revealing, is at hand. The true sign may take another form. Let us look at an example that may be instructive:

A woman patient complains about the sound from a radio outside the office (which actually is barely noticeable). Her accompanying thoughts are an intricate network of ideas that have all appeared before, but not in this connection. The thought that people are able in this way to force others to hear their "private pleasures" is not far from her concern about the way her father intrudes his own preoccupations with sexuality on everyone who will listen to his allusions. She is also reminded that motorcycles pass her house from time to time, making an enormous amount of noise, and nothing can be done to stop them. She is not innocent of intruding herself: she had the trees sprayed on her property, and the spray contaminated her neighbor's laundry, maybe exacerbating the neighbor's eczema. Truck drivers give her trouble when they leer at her as she drives her car in town, although frequently she has doubts of her own attractiveness.

The common element in all these thoughts is of intrusiveness, which we are disposed to take as the "signified" for which the other terms are signifying metaphors. But intrusiveness is an abstraction, and we leave for other occasions the question of what it is that is being abstracted, assuming that the deepest and most personal elements in experience are eventful. Here we only stress that the listener has approximated a variety of more or less unrelated statements of his patient and located a common structure, which is, if not *the* meaning of them, is one of the meanings.

Now how is it that this discovery of latent structure takes place? The speaker is herself only vaguely aware of the connections in her thoughts; she is appropriately executing her part of the bargain, namely to speak her thoughts as unrestrainedly as she can. The listener on his side is trying to hear all the thoughts without showing partiality to any of them, while yet being himself constrained by all he knows of this patient, all he knows of psychoanalysis (practically and theoretically), and all the resonances of his private experience. As it happens the example chosen seems to be sufficiently transparent that it could be understood—as far as the foregoing interpretation has advanced—even if it had come at the beginning of an analysis (which, we know from experience is not very likely, because it is the process of analyzing that facilitates the occurrence of such clusters of ideas). But what actually happens when a cluster of this kind is uttered and heard?

It is immediately apparent that these ideas are intensely sensory. (They are also sensual, but that is secondary.) There are sounds, sights, skin sensations (and presumably smells) that, in being communicated verbally, are recreated in the mind of the listener. They are imaginings. In E. S. Casey's (1976) analysis of imagining, they would fall mainly into the category of "images" and also to some extent into the category of "imagining that"; they are pictorial and situational. During and after the moment of imagining, they are the property of the listener's experience, not only as specimens of his patients's experience, but as they evoke accords from his own history and as he is permitted to take part in the movement of hers. It may depend on who the listener is whether the imaginings are primarily visual or in another modality. Does he "see" the radio near the window in a nearby house? Does he see the motorcycle? Or recreate the sound of the roar? Does he see the papules or vesicles of eczema, or feel itching sensations? Probably all or most of these, but dominated by one special modality.

It is noteworthy that at this stage a transformation has occurred from the verbal to the sensory, or rather that the verbal narrative evokes the sensory images from which it is inseparable. This stage is always present when we are on the way to interpretation; it has to be present, because language always bears the burden of sense experience, for both the speaker and the listener. Not, as has sometimes been contended, that language encodes a nonverbal message that was originally purely sensory; that requires a differentiation between language and experience not intended in our present frame of reference. It is as a totality that the experience condenses utterances and imaginings. They are not only images in a quasi-static sense, but also they are imagined situations (the spray drifting through the air, and the neighbor's predicament). While they are for the listener always bracketed elements, and tagged as part of his patient's memory, they cannot be kept in total isolation from his own history, which for him too exists as verbally organized memory. Therefore they are fitted into pre-existent structures, which they should also modify.

What distinguishes psychoanalytic dialogue from conversation comes into view at precisely this point. Until now, we can think of a conversation carried on, maybe not very rationally, in which one or both of the participants engaged in free association; if only one, then with the other making whatever comments he chose in reply. In psychoanalysis, the dialogue is asymmetrical, although the unspoken responses, verbal and imaginal, of the analyst do exactly parallel the patient's utterances, so that there is a partial latent symmetry after all. The analyst's selection of what he is to say and of what he will keep silent is the interpretive function in a technical sense, concerning which we have little to say in this study. We are concerned rather with that from which he has to select his responses.

How does the assemblage of images—and "imag-

inings that"—lead to any conclusion, whether or not
the conclusion be told to anyone? Wonder has arisen
at the time that such a curious assemblage has been
noted. The analyst observes within himself images he
thinks must correspond significantly with the images
in his patient's mind. Made uneasy by the unstable
condition of the images, which seem to flow into one
another as if they had affinities for one another, he
attempts to effect a "closure." He is in the state of any
questioner of nature for a moment, although the nature here is really not his environment, but his own
world of the moment. Indeed he lives professionally
in a nearly constant state of mental disarray, since it
is the function of free association to disrupt ordinary
continuities and closures, which are seen as defensive
organizations unconsciously promoted against the
anxiety of unconscious conflict. A lot is at stake here,
since the readiest solution of the problem at hand may
also be the most trivial and impersonal. It might
spring from an impression of the moment or be guided
by a private experience that has no bearing on the patient's own, or, worst of all, it might perhaps be the
expression of a theoretical position that happened to
be paramount in the analyst's mind at that time.
None of these could lead to a nondefensive closure for
either patient or analyst.

I proposed in connection with the illustrative instance that the common element of the images in the
patient's narrative was the idea of "intrusiveness."
That would also be an example of the kind of interpretation that falls short of the mark. It is summary, cor-

rect, and appears to be the signified element represented by several signifiers. It is certainly not the
conscious intention of the patient's narrative. But it is
also, as I have said, abstract. That means, in the psychoanalytic setting, that it is more like a comment on
the universe than a statement of the patient's desire.
But why do we turn to desire to find the pivot of our
interpretation?

We can try to answer this question in two ways.
One is by way of the history of psychoanalysis, and
the other is by way of looking at the psychoanalytical
situation itself. Here let us come back to the dialogue.
In the first place the patient is here because she wants
something, "wants" in more than one sense. She
wants to be free of symptoms, wants a helper in that
effort, wants a listener (since she knows before coming the first time that this "doctor" is a listener),
wants either to recover some good experiences she
used to have and has no longer, or she wants to have
good experiences others claim to have and she has not
had. But she also wants to fill a lack, an absence,
something "wanting," about which she may or may
not have some idea. Lest I be thought to be taking
refuge here in that psychoanalytic view of women lat-
terly under attack and now widely reconsidered, let
me add that the kind of want exists equally in men
and women patients.

There is a third kind of want, and that is the want
for something from the analyst, which embodies all
the other wants in the one person. Whatever else this
want comprises, it is a desire for full recognition—rec-

ognition of oneself as one knows oneself, and as one does not know oneself, but hopes to know. All desire aims at the future, and this especially, because it is a desire for a revelatory knowledge to come, often first and naively experienced as the desire for the recovery of a buried memory, a lost trauma.

To speak at all is to express the desire to be recognized and heard, whether the speech is in the form of a demand or not. The act of interpretation has accordingly a threefold revelatory purpose: to disclose the message hidden in the manifest statements, to disclose the desire implicit in the message, and to disclose the identity of the person or persons on whom the demand is made. These are not three separate acts, although they may have to be taken up as separate elements of the one act of disclosure. What is more, all of them are latent in the same acts of speaking: meaning, desire, and, in the Freudian sense, object. And all of them must therefore also be disclosed through the intermediation of imagining. In the case of the hidden desire and the hidden object, it is not a question of imagining, but of imagining-that: a situation has to be imagined. For example, the situation has to be imagined that the patient referred to earlier (by way of her series of statements that add up to a complaint about intrusiveness and a confession of her own) also is inviting the intrusive attention of the analyst, saying, in fact, "Why do you ignore my attractiveness?" in which question the second person of the dialogue stands for the actually intrusive, but also frustrating, father. The imagining-that from which this interpretation grows, is not especially visual, but contains vague memories of someone's own demand for attention and love. All such imaginings need to be confirmed by reference to the actual words of the patient; for this moment, the analyst resembles the objective scientist, as he confronts his hypothesis with the external evidence.

It is also when we come to the interpretation of desire that we can begin to see how the process of interpretation brings us to the dynamic unconscious that is at the heart of Freudian psychoanalysis. Up to this point we might have been occupied with quite a different kind of unconscious—a sort of simultaneous registration of consciousness in another medium. There would be nothing determinative at all about an unconscious that was intentional only with respect to concealment of ideas, and not with respect to the concealment of desire. If my patient were hiding in her language only that she disliked intrusiveness, even including her own, we would not progress very far toward understanding what bearing this dislike has on her personal conflicts. When we can extend our understanding of her latent intentions to the desire for being intruded upon, we stand at the threshold of an interpretation which discloses conflict, and thereby may facilitate its resolution.

Nevertheless, I do not wish to give the impression that desire is something added on to the analysis of the statements of the patient. That would be to miss the point completely, which is that desire is immanent in all utterances, and is disclosed whenever we are able to bring together in our interpretive imagining the relations among the images. Lacan's (1977, p. 167) interesting correlation of desire with metonymy is pertinent here: through the contiguity of images we can read the movement among them, the pressure of one upon another, as a passage of desire. Yet even this is not necessary, since it is evident from the associations themselves that it is desire that brings them to life, from the pleasure seeking of the owner of the offending radio to that of the leering truck driver. What the interpreter does is based on his assumption that the desire latent in the images is the patient's desire too, just as all the images are of her selection.

There is another question pertinent to our emphasis on imagining in interpretation. That concerns the status of the imaginings of the patient. If we can establish the contention that the transformation of utterances into imaginings in the mind of the analyst is at the heart of the process, we must inquire further into the reverse transformation. The essence of interpretation is the discovery of the unconscious relations existing among the utterances, and we get to them by way of their representation as images. Why is that so? From all evidence it is so because the imagining process is preverbal in its origin. What has happened to the attentive analyst is that he has allowed his listening to revert—to regress?—to a preverbal state, and now he may perceive as visual shapes that which came to him first in the form of words. That is, the patient supplied the words, but he must supply out of his own memory the shapes they take in his imaging.

Need we not also assume that in the patient's mind the utterances embody something pre-existent?

Let us take heed not to ignore our position that language is our way of being, that it is not something added to mental life, but is mental life. It is not, however, all of mental life, since there is a difference between words and images. Words cannot themselves be unconscious. The unconscious state of the idea is perfectly real since it has effects that only a reality can have, but it is knowable only through figures of speech drawn from conscious experience. We can only tell what unconscious ideas are like or not like; we cannot tell what they are. Earlier I noted that we have the feeling that in speaking we are putting something into words, and it is of that something that we are commenting here. In the first place it is words too, since it is the unspoken, yet-to-be-spoken statement that already exists in advance of speech-acts. But we have to add to this description that which psycho-analysis has made evident: that the yet-to-be-spoken, which is none other than the preconscious, is itself under constraints that are themselves unconscious.

Here we may well, although for the first time, turn to the dream for assistance. Analysis of dreams suggested to Freud that perceptions and reflections upon them undergo modification long before the dream process proper (before the time we now know to be the REM time). They have a preconscious existence, but the transformations they undergo to become the manifest dream are subject to unconscious ideas— maybe to be understood mainly as the precipitates of earlier states of mind—which by analogy with certain conscious states we have called unconscious fantasies.

In its ordinary meaning a fantasy may be any imagining. In psychoanalytical meaning it carries with it a wishful element. To fantasize something is to think about it in its absence with an accompanying desire. When we interpret we speak these unspoken—but not ineffable, even though sometimes "unspeakable"—fantasies. What commands our notice here is that it is language that is the bearer of unconscious fantasies, which may never have existed in verbal form, but which are disclosed in analyzing from their latent state in the tropes of language.

Lacan's much-contested dictum, "the unconscious is structured like a language," has its roots here. Lacan has always been far from claiming for language all of mental life. He has never ceased pointing to the "imaginary" as the preliminary condition, to which the "symbolic"—mainly represented by language—is the successor. But the imaginary is the infantile mental life par excellence, and when it is reached through language, it is reached by way of the properties of language that reveal the workings of unconscious processes—and, namely, the primary process. Even the imaginary comes to us through the agency of language but particularly through the agency of that language which is closest to its origins. Laplanche's addendum to his study (with Leclaire, 1972, p. 178) of "The Unconscious" is that "the unconscious is the condition of language," which may clarify this point. But the unconscious fantasy, known only as a construction, may yet be the most elementary unit and the most inclusive. It is (1) private, (2) closer to image than to word, (3) implicit in language, (4) wishful. In addition, as we see from the choice of the word "fantasy" for it, the unconscious fantasy is presumably allied somehow with conscious fantasies, which it may guide and direct: we conclude thus from the fact that analysis of many conscious fantasies may point to the one unconscious fantasy inherent in all of them. Unconscious fantasies may also be that something else, beyond what we put into words.

What psychoanalysis, and it alone, teaches is that language through which persons come into being as themselves is the vehicle of unconscious fantasies, which are apart from psychoanalysis unknown aspects of the self. The interpreter includes in his interpretation above all the unconscious fantasies that he reaches through language. For in them the speaker speaks that which he does not know, but which he may come to know through interpretation.

4

The Recovery of the
Past in Psychoanalysis

In a classic aphorism written to Fliess, Freud said:
"Happiness is the deferred[1] fulfillment of a prehistoric
wish" (1954, p. 244). Here in lapidary form is surely
one of the great innovative ideas, as important in its
potential consequences as any of the great equations
of physics or the concept of biological evolution. Like
them it has the quality of being new and yet inevitably arising from a long tradition—for is it not in its
own way derived from the Platonic assurance that
learning is recollection? Psychoanalysis has little to
say about the state of the mind before birth, in which
Socrates was interested, but the period "before history" is burdened by it with much of what later life
only makes plain.

The heavy word in the aphorism is "prehistoric."
The wish that comes to fulfillment with happiness for
its consequence (Freud leaves out here what he already knew quite well, that unhappiness has the same
origin) originates in a period of life that is analogous
to the prehistoric period in the life of humanity, the

1. German: "nachträgliche."

period from which we have only nonliterary remains, when the event has not yet been immortalized in the word. History is verbal, whether it be articulated in an oral tradition or handed down in documentary form. The "mute stones"—and bones—of prehistory do not speak, although sometimes their approximations suggest relationships that imply speech. One has only to think of such examples as Etruscan civilization, itself of a high order as revealed by its artifacts, and yet darkened to historical knowledge because of our insufficient understanding of its language. When we go back to the life of genuinely prehistoric man, to the cave painters of Lascaux, for example, whose artistic development is of such high eminence, we are struck dumb in our efforts to explain their work; or rather we are sent into a Babel of contradictory assertion, and there is no hope for a conclusive answer. If, however, further researches reveal that what appear to us to be only pictorial, mimetic reproductions of animal (and a few human) forms turn out to include a decipherable script, however primitive, we would be well on the way to knowing what the paintings and inscriptions mean.

This does not mean that the written word provides definitive answers to historical questions. Much of the labor of historians is expended in assessing the merits of rival explanations and interpretations; fashions exist in historiography so that now this and now that aspect of history assumes central importance, and the reconstruction of meaning of well-documented events of the past can take more than one route. One can refer simply to current histories of slavery before the American Civil War, which, contested as they are, all stand together in opposition to prerevisionist history, which in its time was also stated as closely corresponding to what "really happened."

The prehistoric past, the archaeological remains, and the written documents of history—these three are among the great analogies upon which we depend, wittingly or not, for our organization of the memories which we interpret in psychoanalysis. From a single word or phrase we may infer through the associative process a whole complex of forgotten events, rather as paleontologists have reconstructed lost species from a few representative bones, depending by homological reasoning on their acquaintance with comparable structures in other species. The residues of past experience are also likened to the remains of ancient cities, especially to those like Rome that have had many transformations, all of which survive to the extent that their stones and ruined structures still exist, often, ingeniously extracted from their original strata and introduced into later ones (Schönau, 1968, pp. 176–87). Persistent, often isolated, memories have a quasi-documentary value in testing interpretations based on current experiences. One scene, standing out like a monadnock of memory, resistant to any form of reduction by new contextual associations, has to be reckoned with throughout an analysis.

It is important to distinguish the three, the paleontological, the archaeological, and the historical. The first two are alike in the absence of the word: the records are material, the presence of the word in the archaeological finds being exceptional, and itself moving the found object close to or into the realm of history. The finding of mathematically sequential dots engraved on a piece of reindeer bone suggests that a message has been encoded. Indeed whenever the finds are human artifacts, we cannot help inferring messages, since the very existence of an artifact may be evidence of a deliberate intention to make a symbolic record. Someone has seen fit to communicate in a more or less durable material a message intended for someone else. The unearthing of the artifact according to modern methods, by which its surroundings are given as much importance as the object itself, is a process that also has analogical value to psychoanalysis. Freud, although he depended for his use of archaeological analogies on what now appear to be relatively crude methods, recognized that the superimposition of levels of human structures could lead to hypotheses to account for changes of which we have no written history. He likened the levels of the unconscious with the various settlements that went into the building of Rome, and always in the back of his mind was the wonderful report of Schliemann on the cities buried at Troy. In fact Schliemann was one whom Freud had in mind whose "fulfillment of a childhood wish" had brought him happiness (Schönau, 1968).

There is a difference between the message of the artifact and the message of a historical document. It is true that found objects are themselves more than merely indexical; they are truly symbolic, and may be even syntactic. The arrangement of found objects may itself be interpretable as giving a statement, such as one of the "if . . . then" form; for example, if one gazes in the direction of the rising sun sighting it along the line of a set of stones, then a calendar date may be fixed. Manifestly iconographic objects are yet more clearly convertible to verbal statements, although even then we cannot expect to have the kind of explication that can be conveyed only in words, as in the case of historical documents. Debate over the true significance of the Qumran finds notwithstanding, the Dead Sea scrolls define new horizons within which the interpretation of a certain phase of late classical Judaism needs to be considered. A newly found historical document effects an irreversible change always in our interpretation of past events and sometimes in our expectations of future ones. The artifact is a bit of the past, unaffected by whatever has taken place subsequent to its manufacture (save by the wear and tear of time). The document is not only a similar bit of the past, but it is a voice from the past, an utterance, unaffected by any posterior considerations of it. That is why it is so important that documents be studied for their pristineness; we want them unspoiled by later reflection or reconsideration.

Dissimilar as the areas of prehistory and history may be, they have one overriding similarity that separates them from personal memory: they have material remains, with or without verbal exposition. The only materially based object that we can use as analogous with human memory is the very recently developed "memory" of computers. Here indeed we do have physical structures, the electromagnetic characteristics of which can be arranged in intelligible patterns, retrievable at will, and susceptible to questioning that can expect original answers, answers not implicit in the question. That there is a similarity between human memory and the memory bank is not entirely surprising, for the computer is devised to hold the data given it and is provided with rules for their retrieval, but only by and for the human thinker who operates it. What the programming of computers has to tell us is that many of the elements that go into memory are physically comprehensible, and therefore that the recovery of the past is a process that can, in principle, be reproduced instrumentally.[2]

The idea of prehistory is that there was an epoch before memory. In terms of human societies such epochs become knowable to us when we learn how to interpret the material finds surviving from them. The prehistory of the individual is also an epoch, largely devoid of memories in the usual sense of the word, although it may happen in the course of psychoanalysis (or at other times) that such recollections occasionally occur. Freud wrote of the "infantile amnesia," and if we push the period under investigation back far enough the word is exactly correct, since it is useless to exert effort to bring back into recollection, or "re-memoration" as some French analysts use the word,

2. I am indebted to Jonathan Leavy for clarifying this analogy.

the subjective state of events of the period. There are also, to be sure, such amnesias from the truly historical period of life too, blanks as unmarked as the pages of earliest infancy, but we remain hopeful all the time of being able to recover memories for the adult period in relative fullness; that we do not complete the recovery of memories is evident enough from the fact that long after the analysis the analysand may remember events never before narrated to anyone, and no one can tell how much of potential memory is never recovered.

"History" is an ambiguous word, constituted by two related but separate significations, often confused: the written or otherwise remembered past, and the events that took place during the time recalled. History is being made all the time, but only in the second sense of the term; whether the events, the happenings, are to become history in the first sense depends on the mainly fortuitous circumstance that someone will see fit to record them and to establish the order of their relationships with other recorded events. Prehistory is still more complicated: it too may relate to events that have assuredly taken place in epochs before records were made, but, since there were no records, these events can become history only in a derived sense. Artifacts, say, are interpreted, but only in the light of analogues; their meanings are based on our knowledge of events from historical periods.

The significance of all this for psychoanalysis may not be readily apparent, maybe the less so because of our familiar assumption of Freud's archaeologizing and historicizing paradigms. What I should like to make clearer is that we work in psychoanalysis with attitudes toward the past that are necessarily derived from elsewhere than our immediate field of study, the psychoanalytic scene. I have so far chosen to examine only one of them. But it is impossible to exaggerate the importance of the ideas of history and prehistory for psychoanalysis. That which has been lived in the person's past is the substance of both preconscious memory—the past that can be made present at will— and of unconscious memory—the past that can be inferred and constructed out of preconscious elements. Such an identity—the lived past with its historical-psychoanalytic recall—is a presupposition of our work, which, however, is not exempt from further transformation.

From here on I shall be dealing only with personal history and prehistory, all of the foregoing being only an attempt to provide a contrast for what is to come. It will immediately be evident that the differences between personal history and the history of societies are very great indeed. Some of them, such as the presence of documents in the latter case and their absence ordinarily in the former, have already been touched on. A yet greater distinction exists in the forms of reporting. Even the "instant" history so popular in our time, when the reporting is done by eyewitnesses as far as possible, or at least from contemporaries of the events narrated, must lack the immediacy of personal history narrated according to psychoanalytic technique. In psychoanalysis all is "subjective," and when it is not we suspect that the patient is intellectualizing, that he or she is telling us a story fitted to a prearranged design. What counts is the uniquely private slant on the events being narrated, and what counts least is whether or not anyone else's view of them would concur. Why this is ultimately so must be apparent from what we have already discussed in reference to the principles of interpretation—in brief, that psychoanalytic meaning is inferable from the articulation of ideas and affects in this particular, private, nonrepeatable way.

The past begins now and is always becoming. Even the moment of capture of the experience when it becomes "lived" is the moment of its recall from memory. Poignant evidence for this fact is the loss of the recent past in senility, when events noted just now are forgotten moments later. The psychoanalytic narration consists mainly of the articulation of the past as it is readily available to memory, the past being all of the patient's lived experience, his references to other persons' experiences having relevance only to the extent that it has become part of his own past. The narrative itself is instantly assimilated into memory (even when the analyst ruefully observes that his patient appears to have forgotten everything of the last hour!), and so it may be said that the analytic process is one in which new history is being made, a very different form of history in some respects, because as a deliberately enhanced *self*-consciousness it includes its own critical versions. The history of the analysis is an important part of the patient's current history, and not as merely a parallel to the rest of his experience, but as it both reflects and modifies it.

This is, however, true of all experience. Living, which is passing through time, is also the enactment of events of experience, and all events are, like historical events, ambiguously defined as "what happened" and as "history," or connected memories. We historize the past whenever we reflect on it and do so in a unique way in psychoanalysis when patient and analyst cooperate in establishing the connections existing among remembered experiences.[3]

Just as all speaking is interpreting (as we used Heidegger's concept earlier), so all speaking is historizing, and thereby is a recovery of the past. In its least personal form, this is a linguistic (diachronic) fact; everything from the national tongue to the intonation, vocabulary, and syntax is derived from environment and education, and hence from the past. But it is in a more subtle way true that speaking historizes in that it must impose or presuppose contextual orderings in order to be communicated. The patient must be able to explain to the analyst the settings of his narratives for them to be communicable. Not to eliminate the obvious, it is noteworthy that the simplest statement may be historical in this sense: "Sorry I'm late today"

3. I have used the neologism "historize," coined by Macquarrie and Robinson in their translation of Heidegger's *Being and Time* (1962, p. 41n), because it points concisely to the making of personal history out of the happenings of life.

refers to the most immediate past, but it does at least two historical things, in that it asserts an affective context, "sorry," and it places an event in a temporal sequence, "late" and "today." Such a statement leads right off to further revelations of past experiences, by way of accounting for the state of affairs of being late. Such explanations or excuses are given in terms of "happenings," intruding or impeding events over which the speaker has allegedly had no control. There may be nothing further to be said about them, if they are isolated events, not recurrent, and not revealed in further narrative to be extensions of a pervasive resistance. In that case they have little more importance (unless they turn out to be the initial portents of more serious matters yet to come) than unmanipulatable facts like the weather. If, however, the sequence of interpretable ideas reveals otherwise, this little bit of the near-immediate past, the process of becoming late for the session, acquires a new historical value. It has meaning, not just in a vague way as "resistance" but as part of another sequence than that in which it appeared. In this latter case, the psychoanalytic process has undertaken to revise personal history by recovering a sense of the past not intended consciously.

Such a banal instance might serve as an introduction into what we have to learn about the recovery of the past in more instructive cases. There is at least one more thing to be said about it. What we discover in our recovery of this element of the recent past is a wish, an intention to do that which cannot but result in lateness, even when being late itself is neither consciously nor unconsciously intended. But an intention is forward looking: it is a plan for something yet to be. The recovery of the past here is very strikingly the recovery of a movement toward the future—as distinctly so as, by analogy, would be our archaeological finding of a cache of coins or arms, which reveals very similarly a past intention for a future action (but of course only in terms of material remains).

It is of great interest to note here that this past intention, newly found, is also past desire. Even when the recovery is of a cognition, something once known and now known again, or known differently thanks to interpretation, we are on the track of a past desire. Desire has been at work in the transformation of the memory, its distortion, and indeed in the fact of its having been lost in the first place. It is also possible that the recovery is of something undisguisedly wishful. All of temporality is at hand here: now, at this time of discovery, something past is revealed, and revealed to be a wishful intention implicating a future.

Even at this most superficial stage of psychoanalytic interpretation we face the question of the probable identity or similitude of the recovered datum with the (mental) events that resulted as in this case, in the parapraxic act. After allowance is made for the grievances, resentments, discouragements, retaliations, and whatever else may be now seen to cluster around the latecoming, so that both analyst and patient are satisfied that a nexus of signification has been established, what assurance have we that this cluster existed hitherto with the potency attributed to it?

Granted further that the grievances turn out on self-examination to have been consciously present, though in an isolated state, in the patient's earlier state of mind? We tread here, although only preliminarily, on the problematic ground of the reality of our constructions alluded to above, and it may well be that we shall not be able to make that ground any firmer than it has always been. We may not be able to know any more surely that this recovered past desire, as now understood, corresponds with its earlier expression or potentiality. I think that this needs emphasis, that certainty is not conferred on our reconstruction by the patient's acknowledgment—"Yes, I felt just that"—since we cannot be assured that this intention, now sure, was then solely, or even primarily, instrumental in the emergence of the lived event. All we can be sure of under these conditions is that we have not erred in positing the existence of such an intention even if it is not the only one. Another intention indeed may crop up at any time, and be supported by equally cogent associations.

I do not intend by these considerations to assert that in our recovery of the past we merely invent the past. Psychoanalytic evidence is a peculiar kind of evidence, but it has quite definite canons, and they must be adhered to for us to claim any substance for our interpretations. I hope I have made clear that our claims are based on direct reference to the articulations of patients and we have no right to impose our own articulations on them as having unqualified explanatory value. All the same, since we are forced to proceed from step to step in explanation, we are also forced to use what evidential data we have, and accordingly at every stage of the recovery of the past the *history* is inevitably a *story*, and therefore in Geertz's sense a fictive, or imaginative, creative account. It would also be naive to claim that our progress in analyzing is also a progress away from the fictive to the realistic narrative; all we can claim is a more inclusive and coherent story as the basis of our history.

We have, as noted, stayed with a most superficial recovery of a most superficial past. In our instance all the significant events and experiences took place very recently, maybe no more than minutes ago, although further examination in the analytic dialogue may show them to be part and parcel of related events and experiences from any time in the past, even the remotest past, as repetitions, for example. So dreams, of which we have not hitherto spoken in this connection, expose through day residues almost equally recent intentions and experiences, while at the same time opening the way to corresponding intentions and experiences of another personal epoch. Let us turn our attention here to the more remote past.

It need not be very remote to be both interesting and problematical. Just as accounts of an event by different persons may vary remarkably so that we have to decide on their relative validity by taking partial congruencies or the believability of the observers into consideration, so too we find that the single observer may, as we say, change his tune. That is, the past of which I claim to be fully conscious, which therefore has undergone only the interpretation of articulation itself, may shift in its articulation in successive narrations. I use different words to tell it, and in so doing I tell a different tale. An account, let us say, of a painful interchange with someone one time carries reference to the other's special expression, dress, or demeanor, but another time to the presence of indifferent or significant witnesses, and its meaning changes. It is the same event, having happened thus and so and may be subject to external confirmation as having taken place, but it is in each of the two narratives a different experience of the narrator and therefore a different past. So far that is of only passing interest to psychoanalysis; greater interest arises when we examine the transformations in the narrative and try to establish their implicit intentions. Sometimes we may find, as Lévi-Strauss (1967, chap. 11) finds in his analysis of versions of myths, that by assembling the story in its variant forms the accumulation of variations leads to the exposure of intentions by no means apparent in any one version of the story. Or it may come down to the seemingly simple explanation that the narrator modified his story out of consideration for the listener's presumptive attitude; in this case the modification is ostensibly oriented toward the present and the future because it envisages the listener, but in so doing it must also refer to a past personage now rediscovered in the analyst.

Suppose now that the heated interchange is not remembered at a time when it might be expected by later reflection to have appeared in the narrative.

Looking back on this omission, we are entitled to say that a part of the past was missing although it would most likely have been available to recall, given the right cues. This is a common psychoanalytic experience. Once again we may come to attribute the omission to a transference value of the lost memory: since I showed myself in such an undignified way in that interchange, I prefer to forget it in talking to the analyst, whose good opinion is possibly to be lost if he hears of it. Or, as likely, the interchange is associatively related to an earlier one that I have mercifully forgotten for a long time. In any case, a part of my past has been intentionally (in the psychoanalytic sense) rejected, at least for the moment. The recollection of the experience and of the very event itself as having happened is a restoration to me of this part of my past, humiliation and all, perhaps. Now with the recovery of the lost episode, I have a new past, so to speak. It includes, with respect to the episode, not only the new version of it, but also the current setting of the dialogue in which it has been recovered. Moreover the "why" of its temporary loss from memory has also now become permanently assimilated to the associative clusters of the memory in all its versions. This too is one of the ways in which psychoanalysis "makes history."

I am aware that none of the recollections of the past so far illustrated or otherwise alluded to concerns infantile memories except by inference. It may well be that the sense of the recent past cannot be established without the recovery of the sense of the remote past; but it is also appropriate to remark that we never get to the remote past in any significant way—in any way that can turn its memories into something more than a collection of fragments—otherwise than by repeated forays into the recent past, the past of the personal historical epoch. The reason for that is not far to seek: like our skin, our language grows with us, and we do not tell the infantile past in the language of infancy (except for those not very frequent occasions when the adult speech of patients breaks down, and even then revelations of childhood life are less immediate than they may at first appear). Also like our skin, our language bears the marks of its origins—analogous to birthmarks, oddities of pigmentation, and scars; but for the most part we are led to confessions of the deepest sort very indirectly. It is here perhaps that the fictive engagement of the analyst is most essential.

Literally, *infantile* memories ought to come from the epoch preceding speech, but we do not necessarily mean that by the word; we refer to a time of great dependency of the child upon adults, when admission to the advanced symbolic world of language has not yet reached the point of supporting the child's personal critical view of his situation in the family. The criterion of the real is still vested in parental convictions modified by the early childhood imagination. Everyone has a stock of such conscious memories, often quite ordinary ones with no ostensible affective value, others attended by intense feeling, and still others marked by the attributes of the strange, the marvelous, the uncanny, or the anachronistically erotic. It was an early discovery of Freud's (1899) that early memories often have the function of "screening": their psychic purpose being to stand for the memory of other experiences that are denied admission to consciousness by the persistent presence of the memories that substitute for them. The "screen" on the other hand reveals the latent memory by serving as an indicator, classifying the sort of memory that it hides. But that memory may be of no event at all, in the sense of an experience that is backed by external happenings. At the heart of the infantile memory there may be "only" a fantasy, which means "only" a signified desire.

Having once again reached desire as the constitutive element of the past reached through psychoanalysis, it is necessary to take our bearings, lest we appear to be making absurd claims. If the present is real, then the past must be too, and we are able very often to distinguish between true and untrue memories. Notwithstanding, it is irrelevant to psychoanalysis whether the recovered past is grounded in an objectively recognizable event or not. Paradoxical as it may seem, the only sure reality of the memory of the past is fantasy—the cluster of imaginings, wishful in nature, in which it exists. This is the point at which psychoanalysis, which has so many resemblances to history, departs from history. That conformity of conceptualization with objective data, sought by historians, is not part of psychoanalysis at all. The validity of a formulation of the past is a function of the coherence of the memories that support it, a set of originally disparate memories converging into a significant structure.

When we come now to the reconstructed past attributable to experiences of infancy, we are on the proper territory of psychoanalysis. I do not refer here to those precious bits of recollection from the cradle in which some people take great pride, and some analysts find such impressive demonstrations of the truth of our theories. Impressive they may be, but unless they too find places in larger contexts, which are themselves primarily the contexts of fantasy, they remain *disjecta membra*, unassimilable pieces of the remote past. How then do we get to the remote past that is truly significant?

Much earlier I tried to describe the position of language in psychoanalytic disclosures. I upheld in principle the ideas of Lacan with respect to the primacy of the dialogue in psychoanalysis, through which every statement is seen to be exquisitely tuned to the imago of the other, which overlaps with the imago of the subject. I also referred to the control exerted by language over meaning. When we come to the disclosure of the hidden past through the analytic dialogue, these structures come into full play. Every statement in this dialogue discloses not only the present involvement of the speaker, but also, with varying degrees of intelligibility, the speaker's past. I have mentioned that speaking historizes, that it actively transforms experience into history, by organizing it into the fullness of the past, whence it may be abstracted as memory in a meaningful association. Likewise the act of speaking unfolds the past, whether the speaker is aware of it or not, because the lexical, semantic, and syntactic structures he uses have all already been made part of his history. *The past is the infinitely interrelated array of past dialogues.* This history, like Stephen Dedalus's, may be a "nightmare," but it is not one from which we can awake.

If the past is recoverable because it is grounded in the memory-language of dialogue, what are we do do with the claims of fantasy? Especially with reference to reconstructions of early experience we are dealing with fantasy, which may have always been unconscious. Since its apparent origins antedate language, how is it ever to be recovered through the agencies of language? Before we write this off as an unknowable, let us bear in mind that whoever attributes a nonlinguistic source to the fantasies we are able to recover must nevertheless acknowledge that we reach them only through the intermediary of language. Let us try to understand this problem better through an illustration of a common enough situation.

A patient mystifies us through his thoroughgoing tractability. This is not mere passivity; he is no yes-man accepting every interpretation without any protest against the rules of the analysis. On the contrary, his compliance is of a more pervasive nature, since it includes a willingness to play the game with far beyond the usual cooperativeness of good patients. He uses his intelligence to reflect on his associations and dreams, not like an expert, which he is not, but like the best possible student, which he is. He is surprised where he should be surprised, provides unexpected corroborative memories at important junctures, and after some initial disposition to euphemism, learns to tell his story with frankness at times painful to him. In addition to all of this he always arrives on time or early, pays his bill on time, and observes all desirable discretion in respect to discussing his analysis outside the hours. He is model good patient. But it is for a long time impossible to discern what part or parts of his past is being repeated in the transference, as he goes on narrating the story of his ambivalence toward his parents—his bitterness toward his father who is too busy for him, and for whose recognition he longs, his entanglement with his mother, which reinforces the least acceptable parts of himself. It is not these consciously expressed elements of the psychic constellation of the family that become clarified in the transference. What does emerge is something different, an unconscious fantasy: He is maintaining an imaginary, very primitive state of perfect harmony, union, equilibrium with the analyst. If we can name this fantasy state with a single word, it would be "symbiosis," not in any technical sense, but meaning the fantasy of perfect mutuality. Assuming that this fantasy has not been discovered by its manifest appearance in dream or elsewhere, how do we construct it from the patient's language? And what does it tell us about the past?

The second question might be approached first, as the less difficult, for we must be unpretentious in our claims. We can only say, in the absence of "dating" references (historical associations that determine the temporal horizons within which the fantasy may be presumed to have arisen), that his symbiotic fantasy, which has always been unconscious, has also existed for a long time as a pervasive and motivating determinant. Its non-appearance in concrete form implies its primitiveness with respect to the capacity for symbolization—otherwise highly advanced in this person—and hence also implies an early infantile origin. Observe that we do not draw on the carefully confirmed findings of the analysts of children who have determined the existence of a "symbiotic state" in the development of normal as well as abnormal children.[4] We acknowledge gratefully their contribution of a concept and a name, but it is also incumbent on us to affirm that, granted sufficient experience and ingenuity, we should be able to hypothesize the existence of this state from the psychoanalytic dialogue alone.

And on what basis? My answer is, on the basis of all the innumerable phrases employed by the patient to maintain a specific kind of contact with the analyst. These are conciliatory, compromising, anticipating, affectionate, propitiating statements, as well as

4. Mahler et al. (1975, p. 8) state that they "use the term *symbiosis* . . . to refer to an intrapsychic rather than a behavioral condition; it is thus an inferred state. [They] do not refer, for example, to clinging behavior, but rather to a feature of primitive cognitive-affective life wherein the differentiation between self and mother has not taken place, or where regression to that self–object undifferentiated state (which characterized the symbiotic phase) has occurred." My use of the term in the illustrative material I have offered, which varies somewhat from Mahler's, was suggested by Rosemary Balsam.

negations, denials, disavowals. In addition we hear tonal inflections, verbal choices, syntactic choices all intending a reaching out for mutuality. The language of attitude, gesture, glance, all aid in confirming the inference. I am asserting here, then, that a deeply buried part of the past, a hitherto unverbalized, unconscious fantasy, has revealed itself in the analytic dialogue, not in the form of substantive elements (verbal images, actions) but in the form of conative and phatic elements of language.[5] My assertion is to be sharply discriminated from the claim to empathy, in so far as empathy is thought to be a kind of unmediated cognition. The fantasy revealed here has been mediated through speaking. If empathy is the explanation, it must mean some capacity for recognizing the mediating potency of the nonsubstantive elements of speaking, for example, tonal signifiers.

Recourse to illustrations of the recovery of an unconscious infantile fantasy has inevitably led to discussion of a transference phenomenon. At an earlier point in this study I have tried to show how transference itself as a hermeneutic concept is inseparable from the conditions of dialogue. I cannot talk to you at all without those "redundancies" in our dialogue that are the panoply of the images we each entertain with respect to the other. These images are historical residues of other dialogues, newly adapted to the new dialogue. Transference is a subspecies of dialogue,

5. It is not my purpose to discuss this here, but such a fantasy of perfect union may be read as part of the lived and living past without ignoring its present defensive intentions.

which is itself modeled on a yet more fundamental kind of exchange—the one existing between mother and infant (Loewald, 1960). To be at all is to be in dialogue, whether the other participant is actually present, or only a mental representation and hence subjected to even greater stresses from the realm of the imaginary than when actual. All dialogue enters into history.

I think that this is what we have in mind when we lay so much and so justifiable emphasis on the transference as the principal source of our recovery of the past. We usually put the case in other terms: the patient offers to us various references to our person, which at first are manifestly conscious comments. As time goes on we are able to recognize allusions to ourselves that are not consciously intended, and with further experience we can assign these allusions, as well as aspects of those adversions that are fully conscious, to repetitions of experiences with other persons, from the parents on. We move in our usual explanation of this remarkable technical procedure from the remarks concerning our person to the underlying fantasies that support them, and then to the origin of those fantasies in childhood experience. The linguistic medium of the analytic exchange is conceived to be transparent. What I hope I have asserted here is the contrary emphasis: the linguistic medium is the sole bearer of the entire enterprise. Whatever is to reach us from the past must follow this route.

This brings us to a reconsideration of the status of the past. It seems a long way from archaeology, at least as archaeology used to be practiced as being essentially the unearthing of material objects and their subsequent dating. It is noteworthy all the same that Paul Ricoeur (1970, book 3, chap. 2) qualifies psychoanalysis as an "archaeology of the subject." Just as a newer archaeology conceives of its function as the recovery of the lives lived alongside the found objects, so we may conceive of our "archaeology" as the story of the life lived with the unconscious ideas and fantasies disclosed by it. But what we seem to have said also is that the past is not really ever buried. Repression as a concept is not to be modeled on the eruption of Vesuvius and the burial of Pompeii and Herculaneum. Just as there are not material remains of the past of the person as such (although he may live literally surrounded by all manner of significant objects and junk accumulated over decades), so there is no need to think of repression as other than a linguistic transformation, which is reversible, although often with great difficulty.

Psychoanalysis is accordingly a process of disclosure of history. The past which it reaches is only that past which is active in the present. Lacan (1977, p. 50) has ornately enumerated the contents of the "censored chapter" of personal history that constitutes the unconscious:

It consists in monuments: this is my body—that is to say, the hysterical nucleus of the neurosis in which the hysterical symptom reveals the structure of a language and is deciphered like an inscription which, once recovered, can without serious loss be destroyed;

in archival documents also: these are my childhood memories, just as impenetrable as are such documents when I do not know their provenance;

in semantic evolution: this corresponds to the stock of words and the received meanings of my own particular vocabulary, as it does to my style of life and to my character;

in traditions too, and even in the legends that, in a heroicized form, bear my history;

and lastly, in the traces that are inevitably preserved by the distortions necessitated by the linking of the adulterated chapters surrounding it, and whose meaning will be re-established by my exegesis.[6]

Lacan's inventory of the unconscious is a thoroughly linguistic one in a broad sense; it includes not only vocabulary and semantics but also archives, traditions, legends, and the exegesis of the lot of them. Lacan confronts us thereby with the recognition that what we are doing in our exegesis of the unconscious past is to make it present in the new dialogue of psychoanalysis. On the other hand it is psychoanalysis that has taught us something about our past: that it is alive in every act of intending and meaning. Psychoanalysis makes evident something that we only surmise without it, that we are living our history in our story; *living* it, making it present now, in the dialogue. But the account given here by Lacan would be inadequate if it were understood without reference to the most effective of all the elements of our history and prehistory, and that is the element with which we

6. I have slightly modified Sheridan's translation.

started—the wish, and desire generally. Even Lacan's novel inventory is unconvincing as stated here. For archives and vocabularies are static, although traditions indeed have lives of their own, and may lay hold of new bearers. None of them exemplifies quite rightly the pressure of the past in the unconscious. Lacan says of the unconscious: "ça parle"; but as he insists elsewhere, it does more than speak, it demands as it moves into the future. These demands are not separable from representational contents; there is no pure desire, free of direction and intention, unattached to a past experience. Through the discovery of the desire of the past, which is what the unconscious is (taken with contrary desires that cannot be treated as something quite different from the defenses), we also discover, recover, bring to light, that the essence of the human past is a pressure toward the future, the fulfillment of desire (which is also the sign of lack or loss in the past (Lacan, 1977, p. 263). In a way man's longing for the past is itself not just a desire to "do it over again" but a longing for more future.

What, then, is the connection between the psychoanalytic recovery of the past and "real history"? To put it in other words, what is the relation between "event" and "experience"? After all, events, sometimes catastrophic events, do happen to people, and they make a difference in their lives. In fact, are there any "innocent" events that take place without having any significance? Of course not, since the memory of an event, according to our way of looking at memories, is a signifier, that is, not just the isolated notation of the event, but one which reveals a meaning. We are led inevitably to the theory of the "trauma."

Freud (1940, p. 185) never departed from the idea that repression—and the other defenses—come into being in connection with events that mobilize intolerable (because undischargeable) psychic energies. The events were causal, determinative, although not simple, and always efficient in association with other causal events, including the psychic residues of other events. The status of a memory (conscious or unconscious) is double; it notes an event and denotes or connotes an experience. To the extent that we trace a present state to past experiences as necessary antecedents, we simultaneously implicate the correlative events as causally efficient. Without *those* events, these experiences (past and present) would not have come into being. Since the events in question are usually childhood events, they are for the most part, but not entirely, consequences of parental actions. Such has been the route traversed in much traditional thinking about psychoanalysis with respect to the responsibility for neurosis on the one hand and to programs for child-rearing practices on the other.

This remains bedrock, as far as the possibility for a psychoanalytic pedagogy goes. Its validity in any instance depends on the validity of the evidence that pedagogic practices of any kind can be expected to have definite and definable consequences. Sufficient evidence has accrued from psychoanalysis to warrant objective study by other psychological methods to establish these causal relationships. Like all such studies they do not and cannot have the subtlety of psychoanalysis, because they measure, for the most part, the association between certain past events and certain present experiences or events. They are associations of the "if . . . then" sort, but the "then" cannot comprise the kind of elaborate nexus of significance that we expect in psychoanalytic studies of experience. The limits of psychoanalysis itself as a normative pedagogy are fairly clear: we cannot ever repeat the experiences that are the consequences of an event, although the event, as a namable entity—such as separation or indifference of parents, birth of siblings, castration threats—is repeatable. In a general way, for example, we might predict that the birth of a sibling—at any time—will be an event fraught with neurotogenic significance for any child. We also know, however, that the later history of that experience is unpredictable, except to the extent that it rules out, negatively, the special experience of the only child. This kind of psychoanalysis for prediction is generally unprofitable and quite resembles the fruitlessness of predicting the future in any other historical sense. History, always in the making, eventfully, as human experience cannot be predicted.

Still, certain baselines for a pedagogy seem to exist. At least no one will contest the claim that it is better—which means less likely to promote neurotogenic experiences than its opposite—to have a happy relation between mother and infant than not. It did not take psychoanalysis to establish this desideratum. What psychoanalysis does contribute is the idea that this relation is recoverable, or, rather, that the transference discovered in the analytic dialogue repeats earlier similar relations, which seem to have preverbal referents. Putting it this way is not just in order to remain on secure logical ground—although that is not itself a mean reason—but to keep clear what kind of knowledge of the past we really do get through psychoanalysis.

The French psychoanalysts, not only Lacan, have put some emphasis on the problem of deferred, or retrospective, action "après-coup," or in the original form "Nachträglichkeit" (Laplanche and Pontalis, 1976, pp. 111–14) an early and sustained notion of Freud's (1900, p. 166–67). Past events—here meaning specifically early infantile events—develop significance that they did not have to begin with. The idea goes back to the seduction theory of neurosis, but it is just as applicable to later theory. An early experience is retained within a narrow range of significance, but susceptible to entrance into a wider range if later events are associated with it paradigmatically or syntagmatically. The full force of the infantile experience—its potential for symbolization—is only revealed later as new experiences accrue. The attractiveness of this idea lies in its support for our thinking that personal history always changes, an experience of the past acquires new contextual experience with the advance of personal history. A present experience reveals something about the past that was hitherto unknown. It is probably no more than an analogy (because of the difference between history as the collective memory of the community and history as the private memory of the individual) to compare this with "revisionist" doctrines in history, but it is at least an analogy. Such a popularly recognized event as the signing of the Declaration of Independence has been constantly acquiring meanings "après-coup." The question here is whether these meanings are genuinely implicit in the intentions of the signers— any of them—or whether they are factitiously read back into the document according to the sway of new political forces. In the case of private memories, the distinction would rather be between an intellectual- ized revision of a memory and a subjectively lived one—and such a distinction is not always easy to make.

Let me summarize. Because psychoanalysis is so deeply concerned with the past, it has been my inten- tion to look closely at what this past is, and how it is recovered, if at all, in psychoanalysis. I have tried first of all not to stray too far from commonsense mean- ings of the past as that which is remembered, con- sciously or unconsciously. The past, however, con- sists not just of remembered events, but of remembered experiences—events worked over contextually. The difference between event and experience is to be sure one of degree, since there cannot be any event recalled and reported that exists in total isolation because it is *told* and therefore inextricable from the totality. On the other hand, there are events that are closer to bare statistics than others and experiences that are closer to pure fiction than others. Conscious memories of the past are closer to the event side than unconscious memories, but all are subject to distortion.

The matter cannot be left there, separated from the particular dialogue in which the past, this past, is recovered. It is a past with special intentions. Not only is it a past that is being narrated in order to change something important in the patient's life; it is also a past that is being created as it is being spoken, under the modifying influence of the analyst to whom it is addressed. The analyst also is an active as well as a passive contributor to the creation of the past. He and his patient are historians who interpret the past, which in turn is always changing as the analysis proceeds and new interpretations are made. The significant elements of the past, those which dominate the significance of subsequent events, are experiences of past exchanges, interactions of desire, all of which either took place in dialogues, real or imaginary, or at very least are only recoverable as dialogues. The transference, the source of the unconscious memories recoverable in psychoanalysis, is the heir of all previous dialogues, which the analytic method actively collects.

References

Anzieu, D. 1970. Elements d'une théorie de l'interprétation. *Rev. franc. de psychanalyse* 34:755–820. (The translation is mine.)

Benveniste, E. 1966. *Problèmes de linguistique générale*, vol. 1. Paris: Gallimard.

Breuer, J., and Freud S. 1893. Studies on hysteria. Standard Edition of the Complete Psychological Works of Sigmund Freud, vol. 2. London: Hogarth Press.

Buber, M. 1937. *I and Thou*. Edinburgh: T. & T. Clark.

Buchler, J., ed. 1955. *Philosophical Writings of Peirce*. New York: Dover Publications.

Casey, E. 1976. *Imagining, A Phenomenological Study*. Bloomington: Indiana University Press.

Collingwood, R. 1975. *The Idea of History*. New York: Oxford University Press.

De Saussure, F. 1966. *Course in General Linguistics*. (C. Bally and A. Sechehaye, eds.; translated by W. Baskin.) New York: McGraw-Hill.

Erikson, E. 1954. The dream specimen of psychoanalysis. *J. Amer. Psychoanal. Assn.* 2:5–56.

Freud, S. 1893. On the psychical mechanisms of hysterical phenomena. Standard Edition, vol. 2. London: Hogarth Press.

———. 1899. Screen memories. Standard Edition, vol. 3.

———. 1900. The interpretation of dreams. Standard Edition, vols. 4–5.

———. 1912. Recommendations to physicians practising psychoanalysis. Standard Edition, vol. 12.

———. 1914. On the history of the psycho-analytic movement. Standard Edition, vol. 14.

———. 1917. Introductory lectures on psychoanalysis. Standard Edition, vols. 15 and 16.

———. 1923. The ego and the id. Standard Edition, vol. 19.

———. 1926. Inhibition, symptoms and anxiety. Standard Edition, vol. 20.

———. 1940. An outline of psychoanalysis. Standard Edition, vol. 23.

———. 1954. *The Origins of Psychoanalysis.* (M. Bonaparte, A. Freud, and E. Kris, eds.; translated by E. Mosbacher and J. Strachey.) New York: Basic Books.

Geertz, C. 1973. *The Interpretation of Cultures.* New York: Basic Books.

Heidegger, M. 1962. *Being and Time.* (Translated by J. Macquarrie and E. Robinson.) New York: Harper & Row.

Jakobson, R. 1960. Linguistics and poetics. In: *Style and Language.* (Thomas A. Seboek, ed.) Cambridge: M.I.T. Press.

Jones, W. H. S. 1923. *Hippocrates,* with an English translation, vol. 1. Loeb Classical Library. London: William Heinemann.

Jung, C. 1963. *Memories, Dreams, Reflections.* (A. Jaffé, ed.; translated by R. and C. Winston.) New York: Vintage Books.

Kohut, H. 1959. Introspection, empathy and psychoanalysis. *J. Amer. Psychoanal. Assn.* 7:459–83.

Lacan, J. 1977. *Ecrits, a selection.* (Translated by Alan Sheridan.) New York: Norton.

Laplanche, J., and Leclaire, S. 1972. The unconscious: a psychoanalytic study. In: *Yale French Studies*, vol. 48. New Haven.

Laplanche, J., and Pontalis, J.-B. 1976. *The Language of Psychoanalysis*. (Translated by D. Nicholson-Smith) New York: Norton.

Laughlin, C., and d'Aquili, E. 1974. *Biogenetic Structuralism*. New York: Columbia University Press.

Leavy, S. 1970. John Keats' psychology of creative imagination. *Psychoanalytic Quarterly* 39:173–97.

———. 1977. The significance of Jacques Lacan. *Psychoanalytic Quarterly* 46:201–19.

———. 1979. Review of *Ecrits* by J. Lacan. *Psychoanalytic Quarterly* 48:311–17.

Lévi-Strauss, C. 1967. The effectiveness of symbols. pp. 181–201 In: *Structural Anthropology*. (Translated by Jacobson and Schoepf) Garden City: Anchor.

Loewald, H. 1960. On the therapeutic action of psychoanalysis. *Int. J. Psychoanalysis* 41:16–33.

———. 1971. On motivation and instinct theory. *Psychoanalytic Study of the Child* 26:91–128.

MacIntyre, A. 1958. *The Unconscious, a Conceptual Study*. London: Routledge and Kegan Paul.

Mahl, G. 1967. Some clinical observations on non-verbal behavior in interviews. *J. Nerv. and Ment. Dis.* 144:492–505.

Mahler, M., Pine, F., and Bergman, A. 1975. *The Psychological Birth of the Human Infant*. New York: Basic Books.

Morris, H. 1977. *Metaphor and metapsychology: turnings of figuration in Freud's theoretical texts*. Unpublished thesis.

Palmer, R. 1969. *Hermeneutics.* Evanston: Northwestern University Press.

Perry, R. 1935. *The Thought and Character of William James.* Boston: Little, Brown.

Ricoeur, P. 1970. *Freud and Philosophy.* (Translated by Denis Savage.) New Haven: Yale University Press.

Schafer, R. 1976. *A New Language for Psychoanalysis.* New Haven: Yale University Press.

Schönau, W. 1968. *Sigmund Freuds Prosa, literarische Elemente seines Stils.* Stuttgart: J. B. Metzlersche Verlagsbuchhandlung.

Schur, M. 1966. Some additional "day residues" of "the specimen dream of psychoanalysis." In: *Psychoanalysis, a General Psychology.* (R. Loewenstein, L. Newman, M. Schur, and A. Solnit, eds.) New York: International Universities Press.

Strachey, J. 1935. The nature of the therapeutic action of psychoanalysis. *Int. J. Psychoanalysis* 15:127–159.

Turkle, S. 1978. *Psychoanalytic Politics—Freud's French Revolution.* New York: Basic Books.

Veith, I. 1965. *Hysteria, the History of a Disease.* Chicago: University of Chicago Press.

Index

Adler, A., x

Affects, 22, 25

Analogy: archaeological and historical, 12, 13, 17; of physical and psychical systems, 27, 32, 34; reservoir of the libido, 42; with computers, 91

"Anna O.", 1

Anxiety: and mind, 35; first and second theories, 48; signal, 48; defense against, 78

Anzieu, D., 12, 13, 14, 19

Benveniste, E., 57

Bernheim, H., 28

Bibring, E., 15

Breuer, J., 1–4, 11, 20

Casey, E., xiii, 76

Causality, 6, 113

Charcot, J.-M., 4

Collingwood, R., 48n

D'Aquili, E., 43

Death: instinct, 15; and psychical experience, 34

Deferred action, 115

Desire: realization of, 13, 21; interpretation of, 41; in transference, 41; history of, 48; and libido, 49; immanent in all utterances, 79; and intentions, 96, 101; and time, 97, 112

Determinism, 43, 113

Dialogue (and dialectic): Anzieu on, 13; defined, 13n; in interpretation, 24, 30; and meaning, 30–31; symmetrical and asymmetrical, 38, 41, 77; and history, 41, 95–99; in absence of documentation, 47; and medical milieu, 62; and the text, 70; and time, 104, 117

Documents: absence of in psychoanalysis, 47; Dead Sea Scrolls, 90

Dreams: *Interpretation of Dreams*, 16–21; as non-verbal experience, 36; preconscious elements of, 83

Ego-psychology, 50

Erikson, E., 19

Event and experience: relations between, 10, 11, 75, 112, 116; ambiguity in expression, 37; non-